Soccer Injuries – Prevention and Treatment

SOCCER INJURIES

Prevention and Treatment

Ralf Meier / Andreas Schur, MD

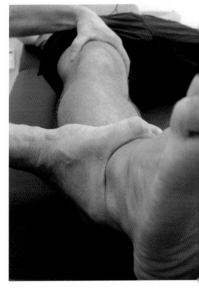

Meyer & Meyer Sport

Original Title: Verletzungen im Fußball
© 2007, Meyer & Meyer Verlag
Translated by Heather Ross

British Library Cataloguing in Publication Data
A catalogue record for this book is available from the British Library

Ralf Meier / Andreas Schur
Soccer Injuries – Prevention and Treatment
Maidenhead: Meyer & Meyer Sport (UK) Ltd., 2008
ISBN 978-1-84126-237-6

© 2008 by Meyer & Meyer Sport (UK) Ltd.
Aachen, Adelaide, Auckland, Budapest, Graz, Indianapolis, Johannesburg,
Maidenhead, New York, Olten (CH), Singapore, Toronto
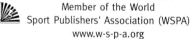 Member of the World
Sport Publishers' Association (WSPA)
www.w-s-p-a.org

Printed and bound by: B.O.S.S Druck und Medien GmbH, Germany
ISBN 978-1-84126-237-6
E-Mail: verlag@m-m-sports.com
www.m-m-sports.com

Foreword

In recent years, soccer has become more and more athletic and aggressive. Even at the grassroots level, each ball is fought over doggedly. This does not mean that soccer is a particularly dangerous sport; soccer injuries top the injury statistics because it is the most widely-practiced sport, not the most dangerous.

Don't let this spoil your enjoyment of the sport. It doesn't matter whether you kick about with friends on the weekend or aim to make the leap to Major League; there are many other more risky sports. If you do ever get injured though, this guide provides a summary of the most important steps that can speed recovery. You will also learn what to do to avoid injuries in the first place.

Enjoy the beautiful game!

Andreas Schur, MD & Ralf Meier

Contents

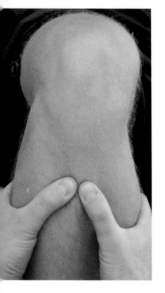

SOCCER INJURIES

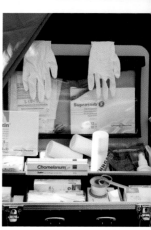

MANY TYPES OF INJURIES

All the external forces that affect us must be transferred through the body. If the body is not sufficiently protected, e.g. due to muscular deficiencies or unfavorable biomechanical conditions, these forces arrive largely unfiltered at the passive musculoskeletal system, where they cause injuries. In soccer, ruptures, sprains and stretched ligaments are commonplace at all levels. On the following pages you will learn more about these terms, which many soccer players will be confronted with at some point in their sporting career.

Bruises, sprains, ruptures – the list of terms that the injured soccer player gets to hear during the physician's diagnosis is long. However, few players actually know what they mean and exactly how these injuries affect their health and performance. Before we start to consider the different types of treatment in detail, let us first consider the definitions of the most common injuries.

Bruises

Bruises are caused by direct, blunt force

Bruises are very common injuries that are caused by the application of direct external force, and are also known as contusions. Bruises can be caused by the impact of a fall or a kick from an opponent. Depending on the location of the blow, bruising can occur in the skin, muscle, joint, bone, nerves and internal organs. The resulting tissue swelling forms a hematoma, or an effusion of blood. In serious cases, a dangerous increase in pressure can occur in inelastic muscle areas. This so-called compartment syndrome involves the self-compression of muscles, nerves and blood vessels, which without the necessary operation (to relieve pressure), can lead to serious permanent damage and tissue death. Soccer players' lower legs are particularly affected by bruises.

The best-known form of muscle bruising in soccer is the "thigh knock." This involves the knee of a player colliding with the opponent's thigh during a defensive move. The extent of instant swelling indicates the severity of soft tissue injury.

Sprains

A sprain or distortion involves the overloading of the joint-stabilising structures (e.g. capsules or ligaments) by indirect force. This is typical in cases of twisting (foot, ankle, etc.). There are different degrees of severity ranging from elastic stretching (strain) to the partial rupture of the ligament and fibers to complete ruptures. Soccer players are no strangers to sprains of the ankles, knees, wrists and fingers.

Dislocations

Direct or indirect force, twists or very strong compression (shoulder), either rupture or massively hyperextend fixed structures (ligaments, capsules). In the process, joints can be displaced from their normal position and the articular surfaces can be split. In the case of a dislocation, the abnormal joint position still exists even after the force has disappeared. Goalkeepers' fingers in particular are frequently affected by this type of injury.

Ligament Ruptures

The accident mechanism for a ligament rupture is the same as that for a dislocation, but in the process, a joint is loaded so far beyond its physiological capacity that the ligaments responsible for insuring the stability and mobility of the joint are torn. For example, if the lower part of the leg supporting a player's bodyweight is kicked by another player's cleats, the fixed knee joint is unable to give way. The weight of the impact twists the shinbone so strongly that a tear of the cruciate ligament of the knee joint is inevitable. Depending on the severity of the ligament tear, symptoms include bruising, swelling and limited movement due to the pain.

Fractures

Direct or indirect external force, e.g. an opponent's scissor kick or a bad fall, can lead to a broken or fractured bone. This involves the complete break of the bone into at least two pieces. Displaced fractures can be identified by the incorrect position of the bones. Small, non-displaced bone tears (fissures) normally involve persistent pain and are only visible on x-rays.

Tendon Ruptures

Tendons transfer muscle force onto the skeleton. They are usually not nearly as vulnerable as injury reports may suggest. Most people live their whole lives with completely intact tendons.

Medical Tip

In the case of tendon ruptures, the person concerned must rest for at least four months. In order to minimize the risk of repeated ruptures, the return to training should be very gentle and above all very slow. Following the rupture of a large tendon, e.g. the Achilles tendon, exercise should be avoided for six months.

However, regular high and physiologically unsound loads can cause premature wear and tear of the tendons, as the tissue has a poor blood supply that may make recovery difficult. These unfavourable loads accumulate over the years, making a once strong tendon extremely vulnerable to trauma, at which point even a relatively light trauma is enough to partially or completely rupture a tendon.

Goalkeeper's Thumb

Goalkeeper's thumb is similar to the infamous skiers' thumb, caused by a fall on the piste or by the thumb remaining hanging in the loop of the ski pole so that an abrupt twisting of the thumb in the joint ruptures the lateral ligament. If the full weight of the coming ball pushes the goalkeeper's thumb back, the lateral ligament (ulnar collateral ligament) that lies across the fingers can rupture. The thumb can then swell in the joint and actually flap outwards.

The impact of a ball can slightly hyperextend the goalkeeper's thumb outwards. In the worst case, the ligament of the thumb joint can be ruptured.

Finger Extensor Tendon Rupture

The cause is usually the same as for goalkeeper's thumb, but this time the injury is a rupture of the extensor tendons of the fingers. If one bears in mind that good strikers can make the ball reach speeds of way over 70 mph, it is not surprising that tendons and ligaments in direct contact with such forces are strained beyond their limits.

Concise Medical Glossary

Cervical	>	relating to the neck
Cranial	>	relating to the head
Dorsal	>	back, lying on the back
Femur	>	thigh bone
Fibula	>	calf bone
Lateral	>	from the center of the body to the side
Lumbar	>	relating to the lower back
Medial	>	toward the center of the body
Palmar	>	relating to the underside of the hand
Plantar	>	relating to the sole of the foot
Posterior	>	rear
Pronation	>	rolling inward of the hand or foot
Proximal	>	toward the trunk
Radius	>	the bone on the thumb side of the forearm
Superior	>	top half
Supination	>	rolling outward of the hand or foot
Thoracic	>	relating to the thorax or the chest
Ulna	>	the bone in the forearm connecting to the elbow
Ventral	>	relating to the abdomen

In Focus

Doctor-Patient Relationship

Generations of medical sociologists have previously studied the doctor-patient relationship. They have always found that communication between the two groups could be much better. Patients are often shy and are afraid to ask questions if they have not understood something. As no questions are forthcoming, most doctors assume that they have given a satisfactory explanation of the treatment required.

To recover as quickly as possible from an injury, a good understanding of the type of injury and all treatment methods is important, as it is the patient who is mainly responsible for implementing them. For this reason, false shame is totally misguided. It is no disgrace not to know what "pronation" means or to confuse the "tractus iliotibialis" with a piece of farm machinery.

- **Bruises are frequently caused by blunt trauma.**

- **If the hard connective tissue of the ligaments is damaged by excessive strain, it is referred to as a sprain.**

- **In a dislocation, there is a displacement of two bones that are connected by a joint.**

- **Severe hyperextension can lead to ligament and tendon ruptures.**

THE TREATMENT OF COMMON INJURIES

Unlike the Greek hero Achilles, soccer players have more than one weak spot. The lower extremities – particularly the knees and ankles – are most frequently affected, but the other areas of the body are also punished by this widely-played sport and are not immune to injury. Most of these injuries are superficial, and play can be resumed after a short layoff. Now and then, a player may suffer a more than serious injury, which requires appropriate first aid and further expert treatment.

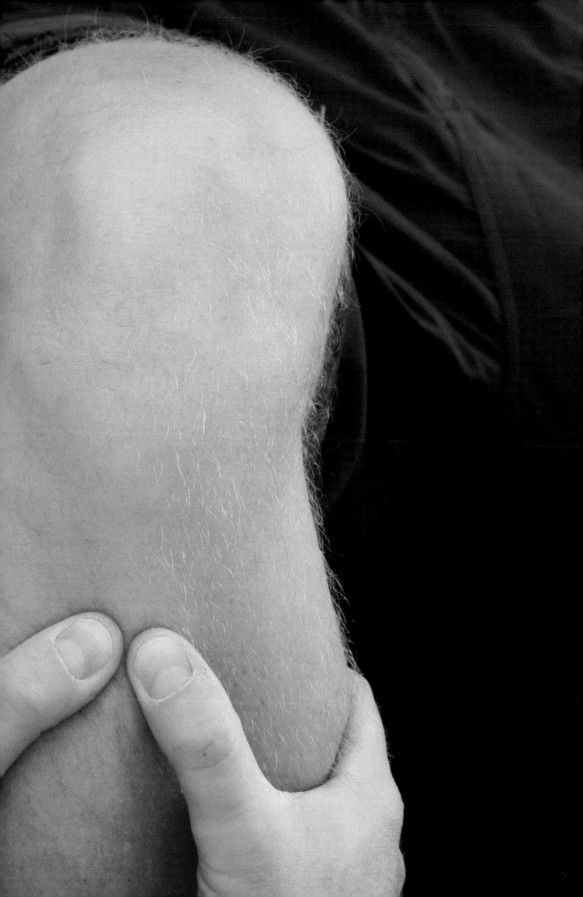

Skin Injuries

As an external protective covering of the human body, the skin is particularly vulnerable to sports injuries. Abrasions, skin detachment or lacerations are not uncommon on the soccer field. These skin injuries can be very painful but are usually harmless and heal quickly with no external intervention. Larger wounds must first be cleaned, then disinfected and eventually wrapped with a sterile dressing. Always bear in mind that a skin injury enables germs to enter the body; therefore a wound always presents the danger of infection.

Abrasions

First Aid
To reduce the risk of infection, the surface of the wound should be cleaned with a Ringer's or saline solution. Then disinfect the wound with a gentle skin disinfectant and cover it with a sterile, non-adhesive wound dressing. Play can usually then be resumed immediately.

Medical Tip

Sweating during a game is inevitable. If a bandage is hurriedly fastened, the sweat will soon make it come unstuck. The wound should also be wrapped with a self-adhesive tape so that the bandage stays in place.

Therapy

Later in the healing process, an infection must be prevented. If necessary, the bandage should be changed daily and the wound cleaned with an antiseptic. Make sure the player's tetanus shots are up-to-date.

Skin Detachment

A skin detachment involves the tearing off of extensive parts of the skin from their lower layer. In this injury, the surface on which the game is played is important.

While a player can slide on grass for a few yards with no problem, e.g. after a tackle, doing this on a cinder or concrete field or indoors on Astroturf or parquet flooring is another story. On these surfaces, attempting to slide can quickly cost one a square inch of skin. Cinder also presents a high risk of infection as the skin becomes dirty.

Professional dressing materials like tape or padding should always be on hand during every soccer game.

First Aid

As the skin has a very good blood supply, skin detachments in which whole pieces of skin are removed always involve significant blood loss. First aid treatment should involve reducing the risk of infection and the pain of the wound. At first, the wound should be cleaned using a spray solution. Trickling a couple of drops of local anaesthetic on the affected area usually brings some relief within a few minutes. The wound should then be covered with a sterile dressing.

In the case of minor skin detachments, the player can usually return to the game straight away. However, if the wound is extensive, pain or a reflex contraction of the musculature beneath the wound can make it advisable to sit out the rest of the game. This depends mainly on the pain tolerance of the player concerned. If the player feels able to play on, there is no medical reason why he should not.

Medical Tip

If the wound is very dirty, e.g. in the case of a fall on a cinder pitch, use a Ringer's solution to clean the wound. This aqueous solution consists of sodium chloride, potassium chloride, calcium chloride and bicarbonate of soda in the same concentrations as in the blood serum.

Treatment
Adapt the dressing to the amount of discharge from the wound. In the case of relatively dry wounds, use band-aids and hydroactive bandages. If there is a lot of discharge, use an ointment bandage with a sterile gauze and fleece compress.

Lacerations

Soft areas of skin are squashed and bruised by blunt or powerful trauma. As the skin cannot give way to the pressure, it splits open. The wounds of injuries caused in this way usually have uneven edges.

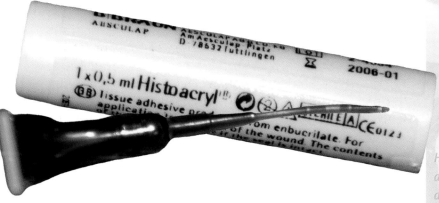

Histoacryl® is a skin adhesive that is applied with a sort of dropper to close fresh wounds.

First Aid

First the affected skin should be cleaned with a Ringer's or saline solution. Next the wound is disinfected and covered with sterile gauze. If an appropriately trained team physician is present, small and medium sized wounds can be treated on the spot with a skin adhesive like Histoacryl® or Dermabond®. Depending on the size of the wound, it can also be closed by staples or a suture.

In the case of larger or deep wounds, the player should be checked for signs of shock (see box on page 59). These kind of large skin injuries are admittedly extremely rare even in such an aggressive sport as soccer, but they cannot be ruled out completely.

Thin skin over bones and cartilage, e.g. the shin or the bridge of the nose, are particularly prone to lacerations.

Large wounds require surgery as soon as possible. On the field, the area concerned should just be covered with a sterile dressing and then bandaged. The player must keep still. There is no need to clean the wound on the spot, the bleeding will do this. Larger losses of blood can be reduced by using a tourniquet and ice packs. Then the player should be taken to the hospital quickly, where further treatment can be given under sterile conditions.

Treatment

As with all skin injuries, in the case of lacerations, you should check whether the patient's tetanus shots are up to date. Repeat the vaccination if the last one was done more than 10 years previously.

Heat Illness

Heat Exhaustion

Although sweating is a practical and useful way of regulating the body temperature, it does not always work. There is a type of weather situation that defeats the sweat glands: the higher the humidity, the less sweat evaporates, as the air cannot absorb any more moisture. Therefore, there is no cooling effect. The body tries everything to keep its temperature constant, however the regulating mechanism cannot work properly in these conditions.

At the same time, the vessels that lie right under the skin are noticeably plumped up and full of blood. This is another way the body attempts to give off heat. However, this process limits the back current of blood to the heart, thereby reducing the amount of blood that the heart pumps around the circulation per minute (cardiac output).

This decrease can mean that the brain does not receive enough oxygen. Sudden accelerated pulse and breathing, dizziness and blackouts or buzzing in the ears are the first signs of heat exhaustion. If the external temperature is higher than the body temperature, heat stroke is also a possibility, which can very occasionally be life-threatening.

Make sure you drink enough fluids in hot weather.

First Aid
If a player stops sweating although his face is bright red, immediate medical attention is required. If there is no team physician on the bench, an emergency physician must be called urgently. Lay the player down in the shade until the emergency physician arrives, and try to cool the player down with cool packs or cold wet towels.

Treatment
In simple cases of heat-related malaise, the player should rest in the changing room or in the shade with legs raised. There are also electrolyte solutions in the form of mineral drinks that contain high doses of

potassium and are drunk in small sips. In this case, an increased potassium intake is very desirable. In severe cases of heat stroke, the player must remain under observation in the hospital until his circulatory system has completely recovered.

Heat Cramps

Less dramatic than exhaustion or heat stroke are heat cramps, but even so, they normally also mean that the workout or the game is over. They occur when the water and minerals lost due to abundant sweating are not sufficiently compensated by drinking.

Symptoms of Heat Cramps

- **Painful muscle convulsions**
- **Damp, warm skin**
- **Slightly raised body temperature**

First Aid

The player must drink plenty of fluids with a high salt content. At the same time, the cramped musculature must be actively stretched.

Treatment

Drink, drink, drink – preferably mineral-rich water with as high a magnesium content as possible. In the case of strong or repeated cramping, an infusion can also be a good idea. In order to prevent further cramping, coaches and staff should ensure that particularly in the summer months, players are already well-hydrated when they go on the field and they drink plentifully during half-time and after the game. Half an hour before the kick-off or the workout, the player should drink at least 200 ml of fluids. As well as mineral-rich water, fresh apple juice is also recommended.

In elite sports, where athletes work out twice a day, special electrolyte drinks (mineral salts) have proved useful. At this kind of high training volume, mineral losses cannot be covered by nutrition and traditional drinks alone. If a player suffers repeatedly from cramps, their strength endurance and flexibility should be tested.

The required fluid consumption in hot weather is two to six pints higher than in normal conditions.

Muscle Injuries

The different muscles in the human body are as diverse as the possible injuries that they can suffer. Luckily, most muscle injuries are painful, but not health-threatening. They are by far the most common type of injury, although this is an estimate, for most injuries do not appear in any statistics. One of these common injuries affects us from when we start taking our first

Medical Tip

Ice, compression and elevation prevent the formation of widespread bruising after a muscle contusion. Start with these vasoconstrictive measures immediately after the injury has occurred to speed the recovery as much as possible.

steps until we die, but does not usually require a trip to the physician. We are talking about bruises, and soccer players are of course not exempt from them either.

Muscle Contusion

In everyday life, it is the furniture that gets in the way again, and on the field it is the opponent's knee or elbow that collides with a muscle. The weaker tissue – i.e. the muscle – gives way under the impact, and the result is a bruise.

Medical Tip

In the case of a muscle contusion, detumescent ointment bandages support the reduction of fluid retention in the tissue. Normally, the absorption of fluid takes three to ten days. Bruises usually disappear quickly with the aid of fibrinolytics, medicine that helps the blood that has clotted in the bruise to flow.

In practice, the bleeding that causes the bruise is usually due to the tearing of a few muscle fibers in the muscle concerned, so that it is often difficult to distinguish between a simple bruise and a borderline muscle tear.

First Aid
In the heat of the moment, after a painful thigh knock the physician must also evaluate the player's general state of health. Usually, after briefly icing the affected

area and applying a compression bandage, play can be resumed. However, in the case of severe pain or the immediate spreading of an extensive bruise, the same measures should be taken but the player should be substituted off the field.

Treatment

The extent of the injury cannot be evaluated from the outside. An exploration is usually not possible as the surface of the area affected is always painful. More important is the state of the deeper layers of tissue. This can only be directly clarified by an ultrasound. In the case of extensive bruising, the ultrasound will often be used to monitor progress. If several bundles of fibers are affected by the injury, sport is out of the question.

In the case of light injuries, the muscle should be bandaged for 48 hours. The compression is only removed several times during the day to cool the muscle for 20-minute periods. In the case of large bruises, the affected area should also be elevated.

Bruise (Hematoma)

A bruise appears when blood escapes from a vessel under the skin. At first it is blue, and the color then changes from yellow to brown due to the various stages of blood decomposition. Along with this superficial, sometimes extended bruising, which we are all familiar with, and which completely disappears, there is also deeper, encapsulated bleeding, which is recognizable as plump, elastic swelling. This form of bruising does not usually disappear by itself and must be pierced or removed by operation.

A familiar household product for bruises is aluminum acetate. Soak a towel in it and place it on the affected area. Aluminum acetate relieves the pain and accelerates the disappearance of the bruise.

Muscle Fiber Tear

A muscle consists of a multitude of fibers that are arranged in bundles. All the bundles in a muscle are surrounded by a hard sheath (fascia) that gives the muscle its shape. It offers the muscle good protection from external forces in everyday life, but this protection also has its limits. Fibers can tear in the case of heavy external forces or quick, strong stretches. Only if many fibers are affected can this lead to a reduction in strength or mobility.

In the case of smaller fiber tears, neither muscle strength nor stretchability is reduced. However, a fiber tear is usually associated with great pain and varying degrees of bruising. Unlike in a strain, the least severe form of this type of muscle injury, in a fiber tear, the pain appears spontaneously. In the case of a strain, the muscle affected only swells up gradually under loading.

A muscle fiber tear always scars as it heals. The scar tissue leads to reduced elasticity in the muscle segment concerned, so that if there is significant scar tissue formation, the risk of renewed muscle fiber tear increases.

In the case of a muscle fiber tear, the area concerned must be continuously iced.

First Aid

The muscle should immediately be rested, elevated and iced for a long period, e.g. with a cool pack or ice (not in direct contact with the skin). It is a good idea to apply a compression bandage but do not forget to continue to ice the muscle through the bandage.

SOCCER INJURIES

Risk Factors for Muscle Tears

- **Overstraining the musculature by overtraining or insufficient recovery**
- **Inadequate warm-up**
- **Previous muscle damage with significant scar tissue formation**
- **Predisposition to muscle hardening**

Treatment
In the normal process, treatment with healing-promoting measures can start after three days. These include heat treatment, ultrasound treatment, laser treatment, light stretching, friction massage (only by experienced physiotherapists), as well as the use of ointments like Heparin or Chomelanum®. After the swelling has died down, the return to training can be speeded up by expertly applied taping. The discomfort can last from three to six weeks, sometimes even three months, during which time intensive loading should be avoided at all costs.

A quick acceleration is a typical situation for a muscle fiber tear.

Muscle Rupture

Muscle ruptures are the next stage of fiber tears and can involve the whole cross section of the muscle. They occur when the so-called elastic limit of the muscle is exceeded. This is called the "self-tear paradox" because the self-protection reflex that normally prevents the muscle from overstretching is completely reversed.

First Aid
Just as with the fiber tear, the drill is: rest, elevation and plenty of ice.

Treatment

The therapeutic measures are the same as for a fiber tear. Any further treatment depends on several factors: the extent of the injury, the musculature affected, the player's age and, of course, his/her performance level. At the elite level, surgery is almost always required to regain previous performance levels. Otherwise even extensive tears heal by themselves without complications, although the shape and therefore also the performance of the muscle can change significantly.

Muscle Cramp

This is not a muscle injury in the classic sense of the word, but a malfunction. This does not make it any the less painful! It can occur during a rough tackle or be caused by something completely different that has nothing to do with the soccer game. The direct trigger for cramps is not yet known, however an inadequate muscle supply of nutrients and energy is a determining factor.

Risk Factors for Muscle Cramp

- **High loss of fluids and electrolytes**
- **Insufficient training**
- **Shoes that are too narrow**
- **Cold**
- **Varicose veins**
- **Infections**

Plenty of stretching helps to prevent muscle cramps

First Aid

The affected muscle is stretched passively, and the active contracting of the antagonists is particularly effective. Relaxing massages and heat treatments with special creams help to reduce muscle tonicity. When the pain subsides, the player can return to the field.

Treatment

The electrolyte balance is important for the contractile properties of the musculature. If the player is particularly prone to cramping, and also in the case of night calf cramps, the electrolyte status should be measured and if necessary, supplemented. In addition, orthopedic problems such as faulty foot posture and muscular imbalances such as too weak or too short calf muscles should be cleared up. Check the overall fitness.

In order to avoid muscle cramps, athletes should drink abundantly during long-lasting activities like soccer games.

Muscle Soreness

These pains in the muscle occur after unfamiliar movements or overintensive loading, and are always caused by overstraining the muscle. Muscle soreness is not caused, as people often think, by an overacidity of the musculature, i.e. by an excessive accumulation of lactic acid. The cause is actually micro-tears in the muscle fibers.

Medical Tip

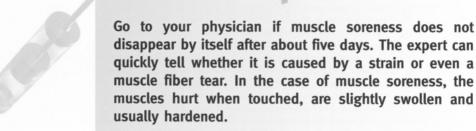

Go to your physician if muscle soreness does not disappear by itself after about five days. The expert can quickly tell whether it is caused by a strain or even a muscle fiber tear. In the case of muscle soreness, the muscles hurt when touched, are slightly swollen and usually hardened.

First Aid
The natural healing process in the case of muscle soreness is best supported by heat and treatment that boosts blood circulation. Tried and tested treatments to promote recovery are warm baths with suitable additions (e.g. juniper), saunas, easy loosening exercises with slow and controlled movements, gentle stretching exercises and swimming. Then plan a rest phase and a short break from training.

Treatment
It is not necessary to treat muscle soreness, but your training should be checked and possible deficiencies rectified by a specialist.

Head Injuries

Nosebleeds

Apart from high blood pressure or blood clotting problems, the cause of nose bleeds is usually a direct blow to the nose. In soccer, this can happen after a collision with an opponent or the impact of the ball.

First Aid
The nostril is plugged with tamponade that puts pressure on the damaged vessels and stops the bleeding. If you have no tamponade available, you can squeeze the nostrils together with your thumb and forefinger for one minute. As you do so, tilt the head down. You may also place a cold compress or ice on the nose or the back of the neck.

Nosebleeds are the result of broken blood vessels in the nasal membrane.

Treatment
In normal cases, treatment is not necessary. The nose bleed usually stops quickly. More severe injuries of the nasal cartilage are so painful that they can hardly be confused with harmless nosebleeds.

Nasal Bone Fractures

The nasal bones are particularly thin and are quite exposed where they stick out from the viscerocranium. On rough contact with another player or with the ball, these bones can break relatively easily. A fracture is usually accompanied by a nosebleed, and the nose may also swell. It can be distinguished from a bruise either because the nose is crooked or by taking an x-ray.

Both in the case of bruising and fractures the bleeding should be stopped and the nose iced. A crooked nose requires expert medical attention or the player should be taken to the emergency department in the hospital.

Therapy
Because in most cases bones can heal by themselves without problems, therapy is not necessary. In the case of a crooked nose, the physician will reset the nasal bone. At elite level, wearing a face mask will allow sporting activity to be resumed more quickly.

Concussion

A concussion is a brief malfunction of the brain.

A heavy collision with an opponent or the ball can also lead to a concussion, in which the inert brain is so strongly accelerated that it bangs against the skull. Of course, any blow to the head is painful and the affected person may briefly feel dizzy. In the case of a concussion, though, there is usually a brief loss of consciousness, sometimes lasting only a few seconds, followed by disorientation.

Concussions have quite characteristic symptoms that mean the player should stop playing immediately and rest for a few days. These include the loss of consciousness (however brief), dizziness, blackouts, nausea, vomiting and headaches.

First Aid
First of all, the pupil reactions must be checked. Different sized pupils accompanied by a loss of consciousness can indicate severe skull or brain injury, possibly even a brain hemorrhage. The player should

lie down in a quiet and dark room as the eyes are very sensitive to light. He should then be taken to the hospital.

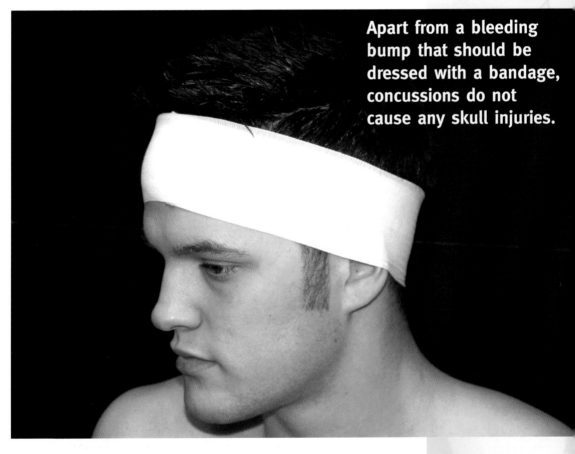

Apart from a bleeding bump that should be dressed with a bandage, concussions do not cause any skull injuries.

Therapy
The player is treated as an inpatient in a hospital since a concussion can be accompanied by hemorrhage. If it is a simple concussion, a few days' bed rest with absolute quiet are sufficient. The circulation is then slowly reactivated. Normally, concussions heal without any lasting pain or serious consequences.

Infections

Most skin injuries that occur in soccer are harmless, just very painful. However, despite rapid disinfection, germs may enter the bloodstream via the wound causing an infection. An infection always requires medical attention.

An initial, important sign of an incipient infection is a severe throbbing in the area of the wound, which is different from the typical burning or stinging caused by skin injuries. Further symptoms are inflammation, swelling, redness or pus. If these symptoms are present, the wound must be opened again and cleaned thoroughly.

In the worst case, a wound infection can turn into blood poisoning. If the infection is already advanced, antibiotics can be helpful. In the case of very contaminated wounds, there is also the danger of a tetanus infection if there is insufficient immunity.

- The most important urgent measures in the case of skin injuries are: cleaning, disinfection and applying a sterile dressing.

- Drinking plenty of fluids can prevent heat cramps.

- In the case of muscle tears, follow the rule: rest, elevation and ice.

- Muscle soreness is caused by micro-tears of the muscle fibers.

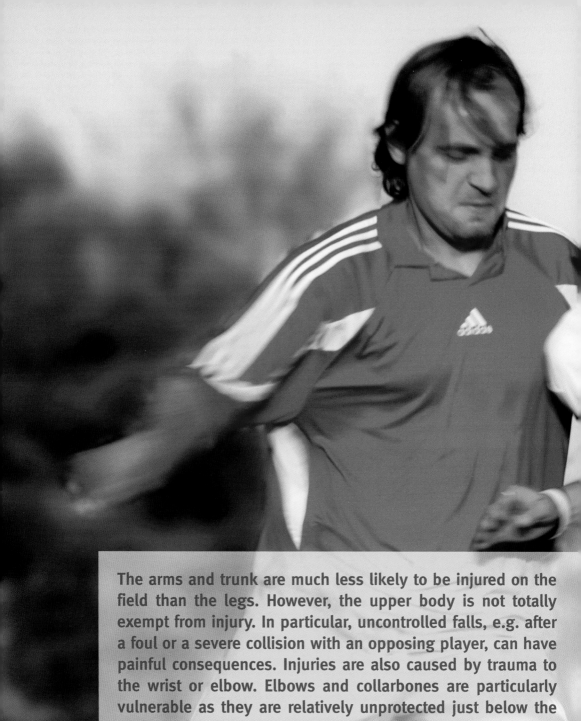

The arms and trunk are much less likely to be injured on the field than the legs. However, the upper body is not totally exempt from injury. In particular, uncontrolled falls, e.g. after a foul or a severe collision with an opposing player, can have painful consequences. Injuries are also caused by trauma to the wrist or elbow. Elbows and collarbones are particularly vulnerable as they are relatively unprotected just below the surface of the skin.

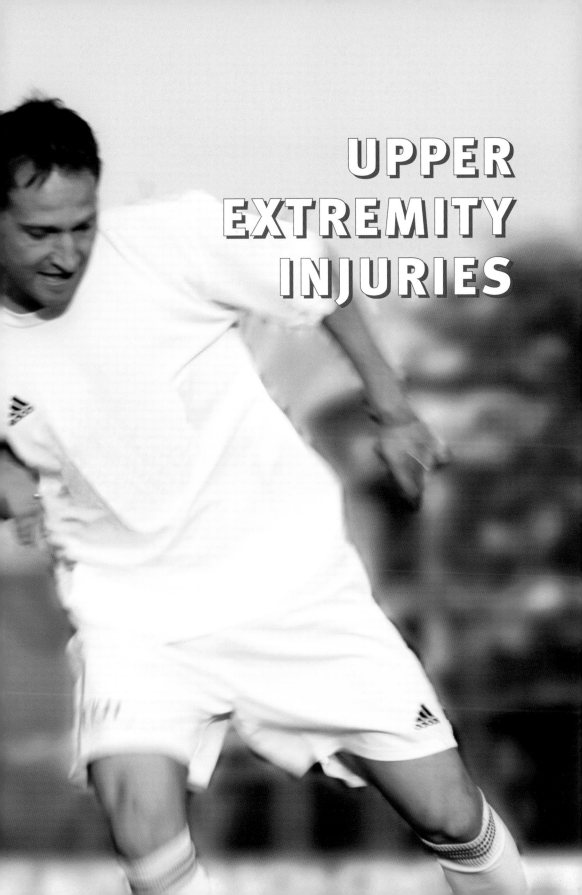

UPPER
EXTREMITY
INJURIES

Shoulder Girdle

Collarbone Fracture

Hard falls either on an arm that is outstretched to break a fall or on the shoulder are the most common cause of collarbone fractures. This injury is by no means rare on the soccer field. Usually the collarbone breaks in the middle because that is where it is thinnest. A fractured collarbone can usually be diagnosed without an x-ray. However, the fracture should be x-rayed in order to check for additional bone splintering.

Signs of a Collarbone Fracture

- **Swelling and pain across the collarbone**
- **The bone is visibly broken**
- **Bruising**
- **Limited functionality, especially when raising the arm**

First Aid

After a collarbone fracture with displacement of the open end, the game is over for the affected player. To relieve the pain, the arm can be secured across the body with a triangular sling and/or elastic bandage. Analgesic medication can also be helpful. Then the player should be taken to the emergency department where the diagnosis can be confirmed.

If the fracture is not displaced, the player may even be able to carry on playing.

Alongside car accidents, sports injuries are the most common cause of collarbone injuries.

Therapy

Standard treatment is to wear a figure-of-8 bandage for three weeks, which is regularly retightened. Surgery is usually only required if a bone end is sticking out through the skin or could do so or if the nerves or blood vessels are constricted.

Shoulder Separation

The accident mechanism is similar to that of a collarbone fracture, although in this case the bone is not actually broken, but the lateral end of the collarbone is dislocated from the acromion. This injures the ligament and capsular system. In a complete rupture of the ligaments that connect the collarbone to the shoulder, the external end of the collarbone is

The fractured area can be immobilized with the aid of a figure-of-8 bandage. This reduces the pain and accelerates the healing process of the bone.

visibly raised and springs up again after being pushed down like a piano key (piano key sign).

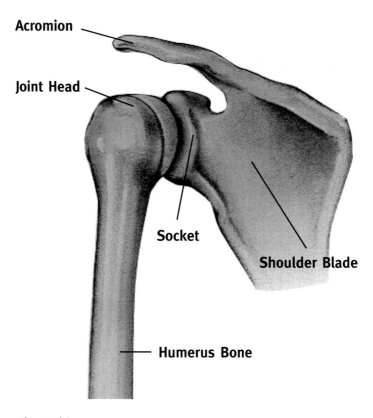

Acromion

Joint Head

Socket

Shoulder Blade

Humerus Bone

First Aid

On-the-spot first aid is the same as for the collarbone fracture: immobilizing the joint, possible administration of an analgesic and organisation of transport to the emergency department.

Therapy

The degree of severity of the injury determines whether surgery or a nonoperative approach are required. In young, physically active people, there are various operative procedures that can be performed (e.g. screws or wires). If the capsular-ligament system is not completely ruptured, the damaged structures are usually left to self-heal. Analgesics and ice packs relieve the pain. Until the area is painfree, the shoulder joint should be immobilized with a special bandage (e.g. Gilchrist bandage). The full mobility of the shoulder should then be regained by performing physiotherapy exercises.

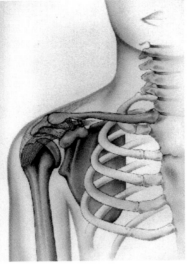

A funnel-shaped group of muscles, the rotator cuffs, hold the head of the humerus in the socket of the shoulder blade.

Dislocated Shoulder

The luxation (dislocation) of the shoulder is admittedly more commonly seen on the handball court, but can also be caused by a rough soccer tackle. The cause of a dislocation is usually the hyperextension of the arm, e.g. when the opponent holds the player's arm against the direction they are running in.

First Aid
A dislocated shoulder – it is usually a forward dislocation – is particularly painful and can be diagnosed by the fact that the arm can no longer be raised to the side. In addition, the shoulder loses its

When a soccer player dislocates his/her shoulder, the head of the humerus pops out ot the shoulder joint socket.

previously rounded shape and suddenly become square and misshapen. The first priority is to immobilize the joint with a triangular arm-sling or a special shoulder bandage (Gilchrist Bandage). Depending on the pain threshold of the affected player, analgesics can be administered. The player should then be taken to the emergency department.

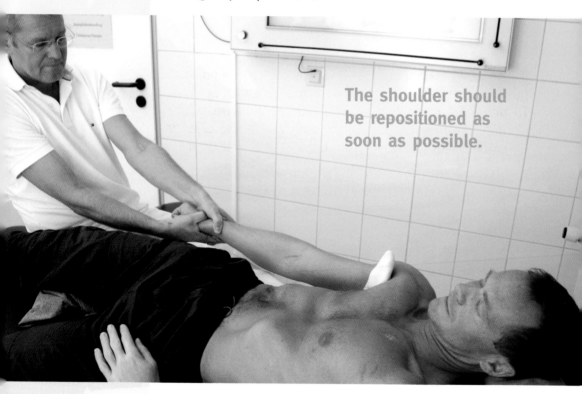

The shoulder should be repositioned as soon as possible.

Therapy
In order to rule out bone injuries, the shoulder must be x-rayed. The shoulder should then be repositioned as soon as possible without anesthetic after administering a strong pain and muscle relaxant. Both before and after the repositioning, motor function, blood circulation and sensitivity must be checked.

SOCCER INJURIES

Training Tip

In order not to strain your shoulder joint too much after a dislocation, you should avoid "overhead sports" or perform them very gently. If you practice golf or tennis as a complementary activity to soccer, special care is needed, particularly if your shoulder dislocation has been treated nonoperatively.

If the joint has been successfully repositioned, the patient must wear a Gilchrist bandage for about 14 days. To prevent further dislocations, the musculature of the shoulder girdle must be suitably trained. In the case of repeated dislocations, an operation may be necessary.

Arms

Fractures of the Head and Shaft of the Humerus

The most frequent causes of these fractures are falls on the shoulder or the outstretched arm. Fractures of both the head and the shaft of the humerus, which are usually caused by strong arm trauma, are quite rare among young players.

First Aid
Typical symptoms of a humerus fracture are swelling, bruising, a misshapen upper arm and restricted, usually painful, movement. As in the case of the shoulder injury,

In the case of a drop hand, the patient can no longer actively extend his/her hand at the wrist.

the first priority is immobilization. Watch out for nerve damage, which can lead to a feeling of numbness and paralysis of the hand. The elbow joint is composed of three different partial joints: the humerus-ulna joint is a hinge joint, the humerus-radius joint which is a ball and socket joint, and the radius-ulna joint which is a pivot joint.

Therapy
Uncomplicated fractures should be immobilized in a Gilchrist bandage. Immobilization for a fracture of the head of the humerus should last about 10 days and for a fracture of the shaft of the humerus about six weeks. Complicated or displaced fractures require surgery.

Dislocated Elbow

Like the shoulder joint, the elbow joint can also be dislocated by a heavy fall onto the outstretched arm. Usually the elbow is overstretched backward. Here to the diagnosis can usually be made due to the very obvious changes in the shape of the joint. Great pain, rapid swelling and a reduction in elbow mobility are other symptoms.

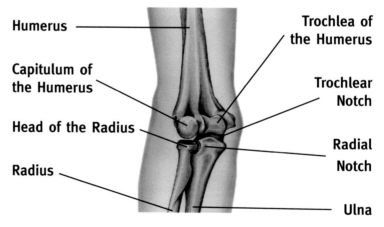

Humerus

Trochlea of the Humerus

Capitulum of the Humerus

Trochlear Notch

Head of the Radius

Radial Notch

Radius

Ulna

First Aid

The arm should be immobilized using a triangular sling or an inflatable splint, if available. If necessary, an analgesic can be administered and icing the injured elbow also alleviates the pain. The player must immediately be taken to the emergency department.

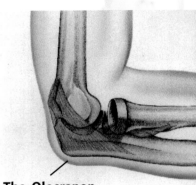

The Olecranon

Muscle insertions in the elbow joint

Therapy

An expert can easily reposition the elbow joint by pulling and slightly bending it. The repositioning should be done as quickly as possible and then an x-ray should be performed. In order to rule out ligament damage, the stability of the joint should be checked. If ligaments or other soft tissue-like capsules are damaged, an operation is unavoidable.

Forearm Fracture

Forearm fractures close to the elbow usually involve the head of the radius or the olecranon. The olecranon can be seen and felt very clearly as the tip of the elbow when it is bent. This type of fracture is caused by falling onto the hand or the elbow.

First Aid

Symptoms of a forearm fracture are pain, swelling and deformity in the injured area. First of all the fracture must be immobilized, and the best way to do this is with an inflatable splint. Icing relieves the pain and reduces the swelling.

If the damaged area of the forearm bone forms part of a joint, it is referred to as a joint fracture.

Therapy

The therapy depends on the type of fracture. Fractures of the head of the radius are usually treated nonoperatively. Often one week's immobilization of the upper arm in a cast suffices. However, a fracture of the olecranon is usually displaced by the traction of the triceps tendon and therefore requires surgery. In order to minimize the risk of the arm stiffening up, once the cast is removed, individually tailored physiotherapy exercises must be started.

Forearm Shaft Fracture

First Aid

The forearm must be immobilized with an inflatable splint. If no special splint is available, the arms can also be splinted to a board. Ice the injured area.

Therapy

Depending on the type of fracture, forearm fractures are also treated by immobilization in a cast or by surgery. The plaster should be worn for about five weeks; after an operation the forearm can usually be moved again quite quickly.

Compartment Syndrome

Edema can form after injuries, particularly bone fractures. The pressure that they cause leads to vascular and nervous compression that is accompanied by local blood supply disturbances and nerve pain. In this case, surgical intervention is required as soon as possible to relieve the pressure. The incorrect application of a cast can also trigger compartment syndrome.

Wrist Fracture

Falls onto the outstretched or bent hand can lead to severe injuries to the wrist. In most cases, it is the radius that is affected by a wrist fracture.

Non-displaced fractures are treated nonoperatively; the wrist is immobilized with a special bandage or cast.

First Aid
The symptoms of a wrist fracture are a clearly visible wrist deformity, an enlargement of the joint and a painful swelling. In a wrist fracture, the joint must also first be immobilized with a splint. If possible, the injured area should be iced.

Therapy
An x-ray is necessary in order to obtain a confirmed diagnosis. Uncomplicated, slightly displaced fractures are immobilized for three to five weeks in a plaster of Paris cast. Displaced fractures must usually be reset and, if necessary, fixed by a screw or plate.

Metacarpal Fracture

This injury is usually caused by direct trauma, e.g. standing on the hand of a player lying on the floor. Although metacarpal fractures can be very painful, in the heat of the moment, affected players can play on as the mobility of the hand is barely affected. The fifth metacarpal that connects the little finger with the carpal is most often affected by a fracture.

First Aid
As with other fractures, the affected area should be splinted and iced as a matter of urgency. The hand should also be rested and elevated.

Therapy
An x-ray will determine exactly how the fracture is progressing. In the case of uncomplicated fractures, the natural healing process is aided by a splint that must be worn for at least three weeks. In the case of complicated or displaced fractures, surgery or a screw is required. Once the splint has been removed, finger mobility can be regained with the aid of physiotherapy exercises.

Finger Injuries

Goalkeepers in particular are often affected by finger injuries. The range of injuries goes from sprains and dislocation via tendon and ligament injuries to fractures. It is not always possible to distinguish between different types of injuries on the soccer field, this is reserved for the x-ray diagnosis.

First Aid

Ligament injuries can be diagnosed by a hypermobility in the "wrong" direction. If the thumb is hyperextended backwards, it is called goalkeeper's thumb (see page 14). The first priority here is immobilization.

A dislocation is usually indicated by a deformity of the proximal interphalangeal joint. If the medical attendant has appropriate training, the joint can be reset on the spot by pulling and maneuvering it. It should then immediately be immobilized using a finger splint (Stack splint, or preformed thermoplastic splint; if this is not available, a wooden tongue depressor can be used).

A bent fingertip is a clear sign of an extensor tendon avulsion. It is no longer possible to extend the finger after this injury. It should be immobilized in the hyperextended position in the Stack or thermoplastic splint.

The four longer fingers consist of three phalanges (proximal, middle and distal phalanx) that are connected by joints.

Medical Tip

Taping (like the Stack Splint) for quick recovery after an injury should only be applied by an experienced physician or physical therapist. The extent of the injury must be correctly evaluated so that no further vascular or nerve damage is caused.

Therapy

In other types of fractures, a confirmed diagnosis is only possible with an x-ray. They should be immobilized in a cast or a splint. In the case of complicated fractures, surgery or a screw are required.

In Focus

Don't Rush Anything!

Several weeks' immobilization is required after serious injuries like fractures. During this time, the musculature in the affected area will visibly degenerate very quickly. It takes a while for the muscles to regain their previous performance level once training is resumed. This long period of immobilization is necessary for the fracture to heal completely so that the body can cope with the physicality of the game once more.

That is why the return to the field should not be rushed. It is of no use to your teammates if you get injured again two days later because your body has been asked to do too much too soon.

- **Urgent post-fracture measures are splinting, icing, immobilizing and elevating.**

- **Fractures must be x-rayed for an accurate diagnosis.**

- **Non-displaced fractures are treated nonoperatively.**

- **Complicated, displaced fractures require surgery.**

LOWER EXTREMITY INJURIES

A player's most important assets are his/her legs and they should be treated accordingly. Naturally, in the heat of the moment, muscles, tendons and ligaments can sometimes be overstrained. More serious though are injuries to the bones, and the bones of the lower leg are particularly at risk on the soccer field.

Hips and Pelvis

Bruises and Fractures

The pelvis and hip joints connect the spine to the legs. As they are well protected by muscles, serious injuries in this area tend to be rare. When they do occur, they are caused by direct trauma from a fall or being kicked by an opponent. In most cases, they are painful but harmless injuries such as bruises. Fractures of the pubic bone, pelvic ring or femoral neck are fortunately extremely rare.

First Aid

If there is bruising with an effusion of blood, the first priority should be icing, after which the player can return to the field. Serious pelvic or hip injuries are a different story. Externally visible signs like bruising or swelling are often lacking, but there is a strong pressure or compression pain that can radiate into the lower belly and the back. The extent of the pain makes further play impossible. Internal bleeding can trigger a shock, which is usually indicated by pallor and cold sweats (see box). If a fracture in the pelvic or hip area is suspected, the player should be transported lying down in an ambulance to the nearest hospital. If there are signs of shock, appropriate first aid measures should be performed immediately.

Therapy

The degree of severity of the injury is determined by x-ray and computer tomography. Non-displaced, stable fractures will heal nonoperatively, but displaced fractures and joint fractures require surgery.

The pelvis is a stable ring formed of several bones. The upper part of the pelvis protects the intestines and the lower part protects the reproductive organs, the bladder and urethra and the rectum.

Shock

Signs

- Restlessness, nervousness, anxiety
- Pallid skin
- Cold, damp sweaty skin
- Shivering and shaking
- Later in the process, lethargy and possibly even loss of consciousness

Measures

- Dial 911 and call for help
- Comfort, look after the patient and keep their spirits up
- Lay the patient down and cover with warm blankets
- Raise the legs
- In the case of loss of consciousness and breathing, place the patient in the recovery position

Thigh

Just like the pelvis, there is good muscular coverage that usually protects the thigh from severe injury. However, smaller injuries in this area make up a good 10% of all sports injuries. Superficial injuries like abrasions or lacerations are most frequent. Painful bruises ("thigh knock", see page 10) are also not uncommon. The muscles are not immune to injuries, either (strains, fiber and muscle tears).

The most common thigh injuries are skin wounds, bruises and strains.

Adductor Strains

"Adductors" is a collective term for several muscles that pull the thigh toward the center of the body. The insertion of these muscles is in the pelvic bone, from where they pull toward the femur. The adductors come under great stress in soccer. The overloading of the muscles, tendons and tendon insertions often leads to micro-injuries, which can provoke inflammations, particularly in the sensitive periosteum of the pubic bone insertion.

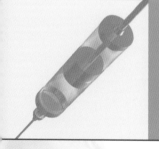

Sudden spurts or fast accelerations put particular strain on the adductors.

Medical Tip

Ongoing pain upon exertion in children and young athletes that radiates into the thigh and down to the knee should not immediately be dismissed as strains or growing pains. Expert medical examination can reveal rare but severe injuries such as epiphysiolysis or an avascular necrosis of the femoral head.

First Aid

A typical symptom of an adductor strain is a pressure pain below the groin, on the upper inside of the thigh and in the pubic bone. There is also pain when the straightened leg is pushed inward against the resistance of the examiner. After a while, a bruise may appear, and in some cases, a bump may be felt. Whether or not the player can return to the game depends on the severity of the complaint. Icing the affected muscle brings relief.

Therapy

The injured player must rest for about three weeks. In the case of chronic complaints, a longer rest may be required. The player should only return to training when the injury is completely healed.

Physical therapy measures and laser treatment boost the healing process. The cortisone sprays that were once so widely used should be avoided, as they do not actually heal; they just relieve the pain so that the player can continue to play, thereby possibly aggravating the injury.

Avulsion Fractures at the Muscle Insertion

A sudden hyperextension, e.g. in a particularly explosive acceleration during an uncoordinated defensive movement, the tendon insertions of the various thigh muscles of the front iliac crest can tear off a small piece of the bone. It is usually young players who are affected by these bony tendon avulsions.

Small avulsion fractures, e.g. on the outside of the ankle, are often not that painful, which is why in rare cases the player can finish the game despite the injury.

The chipping of a small piece of bone by excessive pulling on the tendon attached to it is called an avulsion fracture.

First Aid

Bony tendon avulsions on the front iliac crest are characterized by a strong pressure pain of the affected muscle and bone, which is why the injured player has to stop playing. The player is rested and sent to the trauma clinic for further treatment.

Therapy

Usually only nonoperative therapy, by putting the injured leg in the relief position is required. If there is severe displacement, surgery is required in which the bone fragments are screwed back into their original place.

Achilles Tendon

Just like the Greek hero Achilles, the connection between the heel and the calf is also a particularly weak point for soccer players.

Forty years ago, Achilles tendon injuries were the scourge of soccer players, and even now, inflammations and tears to this tendon top the injury statistics. Now though, modern treatment techniques are able to ensure a speedy return to the field.

Tendon Inflammations

The fear of an Achilles tendon tear is naturally common. However, this serious injury is not so common in soccer that players must run around the field constantly fearing for their health. The great majority of soccer players end their careers with their tendons in one piece.

Also, the risk of a tear only increases after the age of 30, and even then only when the tendon has already suffered several smaller injuries and changes due to wear and tear. A healthy Achilles tendon is so strong and

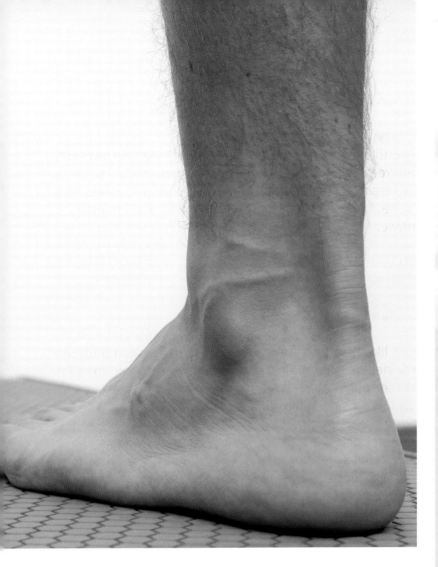

resilient that it can only be torn by a serious accident, not by an enthusiastic tackle by an opponent or a sprain on the soccer field.

It is more likely that a player will pick up an inflammation of the tendon or the paratendon, which is felt as a chronic long-term irritation or as acute pain during a game. A local pain during effort that disappears in the recovery phase is also typical of overloading complaints. Barefoot running also increases the pain while higher heels bring relief.

The Achilles tendon is surrounded by a low friction synovial sheath, also called the paratendon.

First Aid

There is always a very pronounced tendon swelling, usually just above the heel. An experienced team physician can use the pinch grip to find out what type of injury is involved, as the tendon is very sensitive to pain. The pain moves when the foot extends and flexes so that the affected area can be determined quite accurately. However, in the case of an inflammation of the synovial sheath, the source of the pain is not so easy to localize.

The player should come off the field immediately so as not to aggravate the inflammation of the tendon. Ice packs and special taping that offload the Achilles tendon alleviate the pain. The final diagnosis cannot be made on the soccer field.

Overuse, usually caused by running- and jumping-intensive sports, can easily cause the Achilles tendon to become inflamed.

Causes of Tendon Inflammation

- **Badly fitting footwear**

- **Incorrect training structure, especially too rapid increase in intensity and/or volume**

- **Inadequate warm-up**

- **Insufficient flexibility**

Therapy

In acute stages of inflammation, immobilization and rest are the most effective treatment methods. A layoff of four to eight weeks is imperative. It is a good idea to have orthotics made with a raised heel. The heel wedge offloads the tendon by reducing tension.

Training Tip

Usually Achilles tendon inflammations are caused by underdeveloped calf musculature, hence the need for a targeted strengthening of the calf muscles. One simple way to do this is to stand with the tips of your toes on the edge of a step so that your heels can move freely. Raise your heels and as you do so, deliberately contract your calf muscles. Then lower your heels back to the starting position.

Once emergency first aid has been given, the next step is to establish the cause of the problem and avoid a recurrence of the injury, thus prolonging the player's career. The Achilles tendon is usually asymmetrically loaded due to faulty foot posture or a shortened or insufficiently developed calf musculature. These conditions overload the tendon with time. Tiny injuries occur, which trigger local inflammations. However, there are a few relatively simple measures that can fix the problem. Special orthotics can address the problem of faulty foot biomechanics, while an insufficiently developed calf musculature can easily be strengthened by a few effective exercises.

In the case of tendon inflammations, cortisone is frequently the treatment of choice. This procedure has a bad reputation in sporting circles, as repeated tendon ruptures used to occur due to an over-liberal use of this group of medicine.

Reduced blood supply and certain infectious diseases promote the development of Achilles tendon inflammations.

Two-legged calf raises strengthen the calf musculature.

It is a fact that cortisone attacks the tendon tissue. It creates a "peeling effect" on the surface of the tendon. This does not mean that it should never be used at all; just that cortisone should not be injected into the tendon, only into the surrounding area. This is quite sufficient to interrupt the inflammatory reaction.

Tendon Rupture

It appears to strike the player like the proverbial lightning bolt from heaven: in the full force of a powerful acceleration, the Achilles tendon ruptures with a loud, whip-like crack. The rear calf musculature is no longer connected to the foot, and it is now impossible to run, which is why an Achilles tendon rupture always means the game is over for the affected player.

Before an Achilles tendon ruptures, it is usually seriously damaged by excessive and biomechanically incorrect loading.

Symptoms of an Achilles Tendon Rupture:

- **Distinctly audible crack on rupturing**
- **Strong, usually piercing pain in the area of the heel**
- **Standing on tip toes is no longer possible**
- **A bump forms at the top of the heel**

Even at rest, tendons are under high tension. They hold the muscle into which they are inserted under traction from at least two ends. If a tendon now ruptures, the affected muscle immediately pulls toward the other side. In the case of an Achilles tendon rupture, the calf appears to suddenly move toward to the back of the

In most cases, the Achilles tendon tears at its narrowest point. In this area, the tendon's blood circulation is poorest and the blood supply is worse. You can feel this place for yourself: it is about 5 cm above the rear edge of the heel bone.

knee. In addition, there are varying degrees of bruising. The extent of the bruising depends on where the tendon is ruptured. The tendon tissue itself has a relatively poor blood supply. Significant bleeding therefore indicates that the muscle itself or the surrounding tissue has also been affected.

First Aid

If the Achilles tendon has ruptured completely, the diagnosis can be made on the spot with a relatively high degree of certainty. A bump can clearly be felt above the heel.

Due to the compression of the calf muscle, the foot can no longer be actively extended downward. In addition, the player can no longer stand on tiptoes on the affected leg. There is usually a swelling behind the ankle. First aid measures are the same as for acute muscle injuries: icing the heel and calf areas, immobilization and elevation of the affected leg.

In all cases, an analgesic should be administered, as an Achilles tendon rupture can be very painful, even if an affected player says that their leg feels numb instead of painful. The player should then be transported to the nearest emergency department.

After an Achilles tendon rupture, no weight at all should be put on the injured leg. If there is no stretcher available, the player should be helped along on foot.

Therapy

An Achilles tendon rupture should be operated on as soon as possible, as the tendon will otherwise lose flexibility, thus further complicating the healing process. This is particularly true for elite players, who should start rehabilitation exercises as soon as possible. Major League players who rupture their tendons are already on the operating table a few hours later.

Previously, after the operation, a cast was worn for 12 weeks with the foot pointed, nowadays, injured players are mobile again soon afterwards with the help of a special orthosis boot. Flexibility exercises without loading are an early part of the process, in order to prevent the tendon from sticking to the surrounding tissue. Six months should be allowed before a full return to sporting fitness.

In the case of older amateur players, the tendency is increasingly to avoid surgery. What used to be unthinkable – the Achilles tendon was always sewn up – has proved to be effective thanks to a new therapeutic method. However, without surgery it takes a good year before the tendon can be fully loaded again.

> The healing of the Achilles tendon after a rupture normally takes 6 to 12 weeks, but it takes six months to regain full sporting fitness.

Lower Leg

The most common injuries to the lower legs are bruises and skin and muscle injuries. If there is significant swelling and unbearable pain without broken bones, the cause is likely to be compartment syndrome (see page 50). Even if the number of lower leg fractures is declining, since shin pads have been worn in training as well as games, they still constitute around 10% of all bone fractures. The musculature around the lower leg is not as thick as that around the thigh, and most opponents' attacks are directed at the lower legs. Furthermore, the forces acting on the lower legs are much greater due to the massive rotational loads below the knees.

First Aid

Symptoms of a lower leg fracture are enormous pain; the leg can no longer be moved and loaded. Displaced fractures are also externally visible. The injured leg is immediately splinted, and the immobilized area must extend beyond the ankle and the knee. Anything that is straight enough and long enough and that can be fixed with bandages can be used for splinting. Open fractures should first be covered with a sterile dressing and then also splinted. The player should then be transported to the hospital.

Wearing shin pads reduces the risk of lower leg fractures.

Therapy

In exceptional cases, nonoperative treatment is possible, but most lower leg fractures require surgery, as this allows the neighboring joints to be moved sooner, thus avoiding excessive muscular degeneration.

In Focus

Causes and Effects

If a player frequently suffers from thigh muscle strains, a thorough examination of the lumbar spine is advisable, as this is the source of the lower extremities' nerve stimuli. Any disturbance to this process, e.g. by damage to a vertebral disk, eventually jeopardizes the function of the thigh musculature. Of course, complaints are not always caused by a prolapsed disk. Even a slight swelling (pre-stage of the prolapse) of the tissue can irritate the surrounding nerves so much that the tension of the musculature is altered. Anyone suffering from an actual prolapsed disk would never dream of putting on their soccer cleats!

- Strong muscles protect the pelvis and the thighs from serious injury.

- Wear and tear damage can often lead to Achilles tendon ruptures.

- A heel wedge relieves the pain of an Achilles tendon inflammation.

- A well-trained calf muscle takes the pressure off the Achilles tendon.

- Shin pads prevent lower leg injuries.

PROBLEM AREAS IN THE KNEE, ANKLE AND FOOT

The already vulnerable knee joint comes in for some rough treatment on the soccer field. Knee injuries have caused the retirement of many a soccer player. Wear and tear symptoms are just as responsible for this as collisions with an opponent. Short sprints and abrupt stopping movements are also the bane of the knee joint. On the pages that follow, we show the most common knee and foot injuries in soccer as well as proven therapeutic measures.

Knee Joint

The knee, along with the ankle, is the most frequently affected by soccer injuries, because of the structure and biomechanics of the joint. The knee is a hinge joint with extremely limited lateral flexibility that connects the thigh and the lower leg. As the articular surface of the femur is round and therefore not optimally adapted to the flat end of the tibia, the internal and external menisci act as both buffers and stabilizers. Lateral stability is provided by the medial and lateral collateral ligaments.

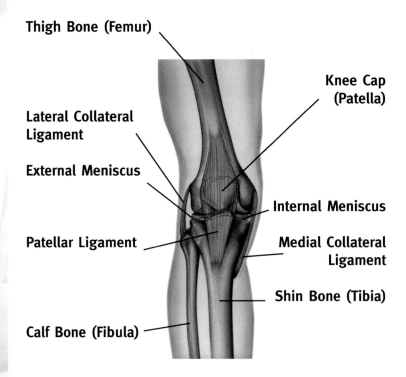

Thigh Bone (Femur)

Knee Cap (Patella)

Lateral Collateral Ligament

External Meniscus

Internal Meniscus

Patellar Ligament

Medial Collateral Ligament

Shin Bone (Tibia)

Calf Bone (Fibula)

They prevent the hyperextension of the knee when straightened and also the twisting of the lower leg. Inside the joint, the anterior and posterior cruciate ligaments are connected to the tibia and ensure stability during twisting motion. The patella, the quadriceps tendons and the patellar ligament all prevent hyperextension.

Internal Knee Trauma

The term internal knee trauma covers several knee injuries. This is because knee injuries are not always easy to distinguish from each other. Internal knee trauma include the rupture of the anterior and posterior cruciate ligaments, the rupture of the menisci and the popping out of a piece of cartilage.

The knee joint is very stable in the fully-extended state, when the ligaments and muscles are contracted. However, when the knee is bent, the ligaments relax and the joint becomes vulnerable. Direct trauma due to a fall or a kick and twisting movements with a fixed foot are consequently among the most frequent causes of knee injuries.

Bruising and Sprains

Bruises and sprains of the knee are very common, but luckily they are harmless, minor injuries. While bruises are caused by direct trauma like a kick or a fall, sprains are the result of excessive twisting of the knee.

A symptom of a bruise or sprain is a pronounced swelling of the knee.

Both are very painful, and are usually accompanied by swelling, blood effusions and restricted movement, which can be symptoms of more serious bone or ligament injuries. This can already be determined on the field by a team doctor or physiotherapist with appropriate experience.

First Aid
Ice the knee immediately; and then apply a sports cream and compression. If the knee joint is sufficiently stable, and pain relief has been effective, the player can grit his teeth and return to the field to continue playing.

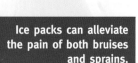
Ice packs can alleviate the pain of both bruises and sprains.

Therapy
Apparently harmless injuries can afterwards occasionally turn out to be more serious. If you are unable to shake off a complaint, visit a sports doctor or surgeon. Often, internal bleeding in the joint is not noticeable until hours after the injury. This internal bleeding can indicate internal knee damage, e.g. a cruciate ligament rupture.

Lateral Ligament Injuries

Pushing out and simultaneously twisting the lower leg is very stressful for the medial collateral ligament, whereas injuries to the lateral collateral ligament occur when the lower leg is twisted inward. In most cases the lateral ligaments are strained and the insertion points are particularly painful. In the case of excessive external force, the ligaments can even rupture.

First Aid
Routine treatment is icing and the application of a compression bandage. A strain can be distinguished

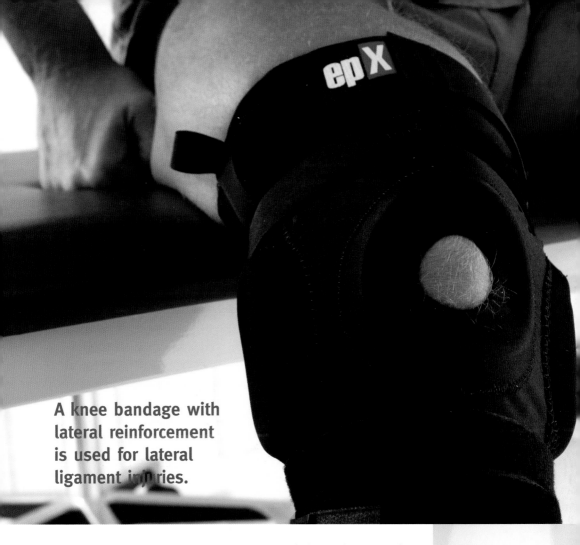

A knee bandage with lateral reinforcement is used for lateral ligament injuries.

from a rupture by testing lateral stability. That can be done immediately on the spot. In the case of a rupture, the knee joint can either bend outward (rupture of the medial collateral ligament) or inward (rupture of the lateral collateral ligament). Further symptoms for a rupture are swelling and pain.

Therapy
Intra-articular ligament ruptures can be painful for up to six weeks. In severe cases, immobilization in a mobile splint should be considered. This is also the treatment of choice for isolated ruptures. Surgery is only required when the lateral ligament is torn from the bone.

Cruciate Ligament Rupture

The rupture of the anterior cruciate ligament is one of the most well-known and serious injuries, and it has meant a premature retirement for many a prominent soccer player. In contrast, the posterior cruciate ligament is one of the strongest ligaments in the human body and is extremely rarely affected by injury.

Direct trauma due to an opponent's tackle is very rarely the cause of a cruciate ligament rupture. The cause is much more likely to be a twisted knee when the foot is fixed, e.g. if the opponent blocks a player's foot while centrifugal force moves the rest of the body in the opposite direction. If the anterior cruciate ligament is ruptured, the tibia can be displaced forward against the thigh bone when the knee is bent. The injured player has a distinct feeling of instability.

Articular Effusion

In an articular effusion there is increased fluid inside a joint. Synovial fluid seeps into the joint causing a blood effusion (hemarthrosis) or pus, making the joint swell painfully. A cruciate ligament rupture is usually accompanied by an articular effusion in the knee joint.

The rupture of a cruciate ligament is always accompanied by bleeding within the joint, which is often delayed until a few hours after the accident and is often not detectable until the following day. As a rule of thumb, blood in the joint indicates a cruciate ligament rupture unless an arthroscopy or MRI proves otherwise.

First Aid

As for a lateral ligament rupture, the knee is iced and offloaded using a compression bandage. The severity of the injury makes it impossible for the player to participate further in the game. The injured player must immediately be sent to the emergency department, and intra-articular bleeding should be tested for the day after.

Training Tip

Warm up your muscles well before any sporting activity. The risk of injury also decreases significantly by improving coordination, e.g. with the aid of jumping or running drills. Strong, well-trained leg muscles also protect the cruciate ligaments.

Therapy

An arthroscopy ("key-hole surgery") gives a clear idea of the extent of the injury. Unlike the MRI or computer tomography, it not only provides static images but also allows mechanical stability to be checked, enabling the diagnosis of longitudinal and partial ruptures. Partial ruptures do not cause joint instability, unlike complete ruptures, where the cruciate ligament usually breaks at the upper insertion with the femur. In complex injuries, the medial meniscus and medial collateral ligament are also damaged.

An arthroscopy is performed with an arthroscope, which has several lenses, a light and a flushing and extraction system.

Along with the classic cruciate ligament suture, in which the ruptured ligament is sewn back onto the place where it was torn off the bone, the modern ersatz plastic technique is gaining in popularity. In this process, the ruptured cruciate ligament is completely replaced by a

The knee joint is temporarily fitted with special mobile splints (orthoses) after a cruciate ligament rupture.

piece of the patellar ligament or semitendinosus tendon (little-used tendon in the thigh). The exchanged tendon is anchored to the bones during an arthroscopy. As an ersatz plastic leads to very good long-term results, it is the type of surgery usually chosen by athletes.

Long phases of complete immobilization are avoided in modern aftercare practice. Quite early on, mobile splints (orthoses) are used, which allow movement within a restricted radius, e.g. flexion between 10º and 90º, so that the sutured ligament is not overstrained but the mobility of the joint is retained.

It is particularly important to perform regular physiotherapy exercises for strength, coordination and flexibility. After about six weeks, full loading should normally be possible without crutches. At least at grassroots level, training should not be resumed for at least three months.

SOCCER INJURIES

Meniscus

It is almost exclusively the medial meniscus that is affected by injury, as it cannot give way in rotational movements due to its firm connection with the medial collateral ligament. Meniscus ruptures are only likely if there is previous tissue damage due to wear and tear. The meniscus consists of a cartilage-like tissue that is poorly supplied with blood. This poor nutrient supply means that wear and tear is not unusual even in 20-year-olds.

> The meniscus is a half-moon-shaped cartilage. Every knee contains a medial and lateral meniscus.

Classification of Meniscus Injuries

- **Depending on Location**
  Front Third
  Middle Third
  Back Third

- **Depending on Type of Rupture**
  Vertical
  Horizontal
  Diagonal
  Basket-handle Shaped
  Lobe Shaped

First Aid
The injured area is iced. Symptoms of a meniscus injury are mechanical blocks in the knee as well as clicking and cracking. A pressure pain over the medial intra-articular space on rotation of the lower leg indicates a rupture of the medial meniscus. The player should be transported to the hospital for further treatment.

Therapy
In order to rule out bone injuries, the knee must be x-rayed. If a rupture is suspected, an exact diagnosis is carried

out with an arthroscope. If the pieces of meniscus torn off are relatively well-supplied with blood near the capsule, the rupture can be sutured during the actual arthroscopy. This is rarely the case, though. Usually the rupture is a consequence of damage due to wear and tear and affects the part of the meniscus that has a poor blood supply. In this case, the only possibility during the arthroscopy is the removal of the ruptured meniscus fragments. If there are no serious secondary injuries, and only a little tissue is removed, training can be resumed quite soon (after four weeks).

Patellar Injuries

Patellar fractures and dislocations must be distinguished from common bruises. While bruises and fractures are caused by falls or collisions with other players, dislocations (patellar luxations) are rarely caused by accidents alone. In most cases, there is already a corresponding predisposition to muscular imbalances or a patella deformity. In the case of dislocations, the patella pops laterally out of place. This is frequently accompanied by the popping out of the cartilage and intra-articular bleeding.

Symptoms of a Patellar Luxation

- **Clearly visible deformed patella**

- **Swelling of the knee**

- **Great pain**

- **The knee can no longer be moved**

SOCCER INJURIES

First Aid

In the case of bruises, dislocations and fractures the knee is iced and then immobilized with a splint. In the case of a suspected fracture or dislocation, the player should be taken to the hospital.

Therapy

If cartilage tissue is affected and the knee extensor system is largely stable, the patella is just put back into place, usually under anaesthetic. If there is a lot of swelling, the joint is punctured. The knee is then immobilized for three to six weeks.

Symptoms of a Patellar Fracture

- **Immediate pain**
- **Significant swelling at the front of the knee**
- **The leg can no longer bear weight**
- **The knee can no longer be straightened**

We differentiate between longitudinal and diagonal patellar fractures. The latter are particularly serious, as there is traction by the quadriceps tendon from one side and by the patellar tendon on the other side, which causes the fractured area to separate. The fracture can usually be felt from outside and requires immediate surgery. However, non-displaced longitudinal fractures can be treated conservatively; the fracture can heal in a cast without surgery.

A patellar fracture is usually the result of a heavy fall on the bent knee.

In most cases, the knee joint need only be completely immobilized for a short period. Physiotherapy exercises, especially training of the thigh musculature, should be introduced as soon as possible.

Ankle and Foot

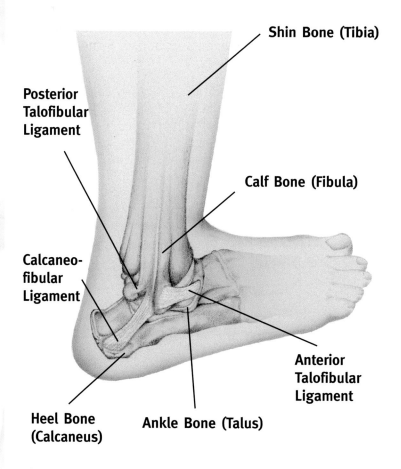

Shin Bone (Tibia)

Posterior Talofibular Ligament

Calf Bone (Fibula)

Calcaneo-fibular Ligament

Anterior Talofibular Ligament

Heel Bone (Calcaneus)

Ankle Bone (Talus)

The upper ankle joint connects the shinbone and the calf bone (tibia and fibula) to the ankle bone. It is a hinge joint that allows the end of the foot to lower (flexion) and raise (extension). A strong ligament and capsular system stabilizes the joint and prevents the foot from tilting. The ankle joint enables a fluid gait.

Bruises and Strains

The ankle joint is usually affected by bruises and strains that are caused by direct or indirect external forces, but which do not involve ligaments or bones. Symptoms are swelling and blood effusions.

Nutritional Tip

Soccer players require an increased intake of antioxidants. Oxidative stress increases with the high oxygen uptake during physical activity. Antioxidants (e.g. vitamins C and E) protect the body from the free radicals this can cause.

First Aid
First of all the leg should be rested, the joint should be iced and an elastic support bandage applied. Often a noticeable improvement in the symptoms occurs after only a few minutes. If the pain is tolerable, the game or workout can be resumed.

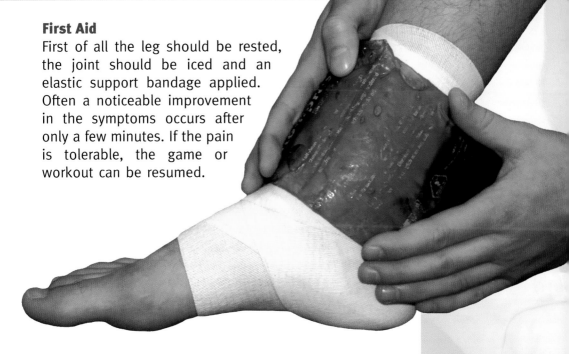

Therapy

Elevate the foot and ice again to make the swelling go down. Special sports creams promote the healing process. If these measures are not enough to immediately alleviate the pain, an x-ray examination is recommended in order to rule out bone and particularly ligament injury.

Ligament Ruptures

This injury is caused by twisting the ankle and it nearly always affects all three lateral ligaments, which extend from the lateral malleolus to the ankle and heel bone. Depending on the severity of the injury, one, two or three ligaments can be ruptured.

Symptoms of a Lateral Ligament Rupture

- **Rapid, significant swelling**
- **Blood effusion**
- **Pain**
- **No weight can be put on the foot**
- **The ankle "spreads out": the articular surfaces separate when the foot is turned inward**

First Aid

The same emergency measures are used for both bruises and sprains: rest and elevate the foot and if possible, splint it. Icing the joint alleviates the pain and reduces the swelling. The injured player should be transported to the hospital for further treatment.

Young athletes are more frequently affected by lateral ligament ruptures, while older people are more likely to suffer from a lateral malleolus fracture.

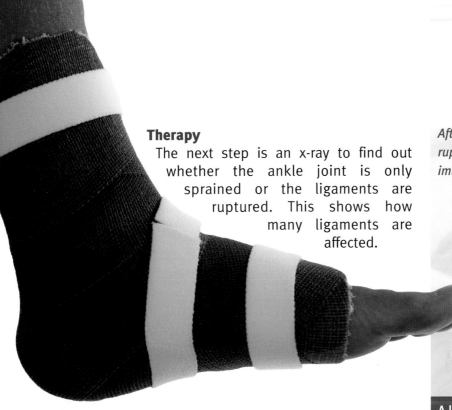

Therapy

The next step is an x-ray to find out whether the ankle joint is only sprained or the ligaments are ruptured. This shows how many ligaments are affected.

After a ligament rupture, the ankle is immobilized in a cast.

An x-ray examination should take place as soon as possible to enable the correct treatment to be provided, thereby avoiding later complications (e.g. chronic instability or premature arthrosis).

A lateral ligament rupture does not usually require surgery.

While in the past, ligament ruptures were usually operated on, nowadays the treatment tends to be conservative. In the case of massive swelling and great pain, immobilization in a cast is recommended. Underarm crutches further ensure that no weight is put on the joint. After about 14 days, when the swelling has completely gone down, an orthosis such as an Aircast® splint must be worn for four weeks. If there is no more pain, the foot can be fully loaded, but if the pain has not yet disappeared, the foot should be immobilized for six weeks in an orthosis.

Training can then be resumed. However, in the first training phase (at least six weeks long) an orthosis must be worn, as it takes at least three months until the ligaments can be fully loaded again.

A consistent therapy is not only important from the point of view of the future sporting career. Without these measures, the ligaments will not be adequately stabilized, and the ankle can soon be twisted again even for the slightest reason. In addition, constant improper biomechanical stress in the joint causes a premature cartilage wear and tear (arthrosis) that will eventually deteriorate.

Malleolar Fracture

If the foot is subject to stronger trauma than in the case of a sprain or a ligament rupture, bone fractures can occur. Malleolar fractures are the most commonly seen bone injury in the sports doctor's consulting room. Depending on which part of the ankle is affected by the injury, there are different types of ankle fracture.

Classification of Ankle Fractures

1. **Lateral Malleolar Fracture**
   Weber A Fracture
   Weber B Fracture
   Weber C Fracture
2. **Isolated Medial Malleolar Fracture**
3. **Lateral and Medial Malleolar Fracture (Bimalleolar Ankle Fracture)**
4. **Lateral Malleolar Fracture, Medial Malleolar Fracture and Avulsion Fracture of the Posterior Malleolus (Trimalleolar Ankle Fracture)**

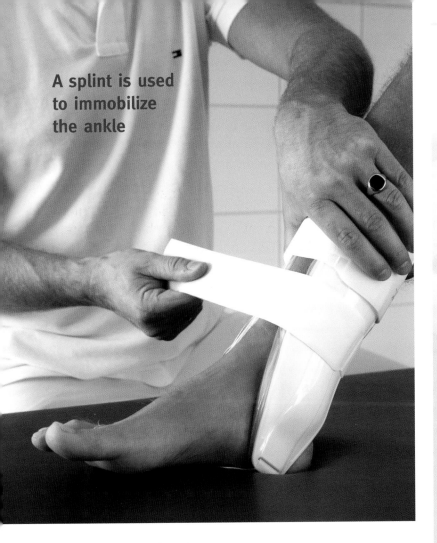

A splint is used to immobilize the ankle

Lateral Malleolar Fracture

First Aid

There is usually significant pain and swelling with blood effusion. Sometimes, there is a clearly visible deformity. Movement and resilience are greatly restricted by a lateral malleolus fracture, and the player cannot return to the game. The ankle must immediately be iced and immobilized in an air splint or an Aircast® splint. The weight must then be taken off the foot. The injured player must be taken to the emergency department and x-rayed there.

Coordination exercises reduce the risk of a lateral malleolar fracture.

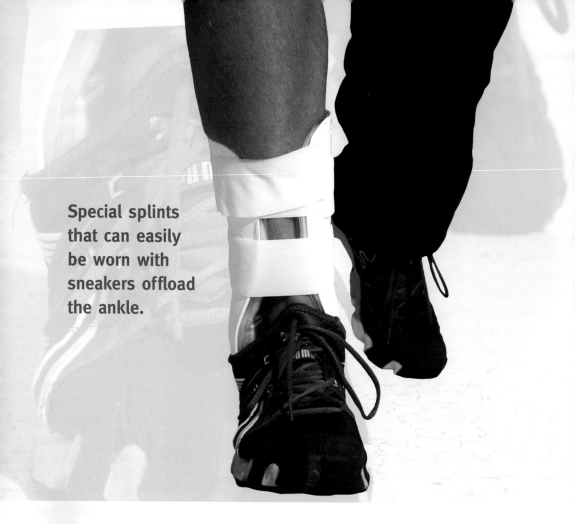

Special splints
that can easily
be worn with
sneakers offload
the ankle.

Therapy

Weber A fractures usually involve a non-displaced fracture in the area of the lateral malleolus, and treatment is usually conservative. If the swelling is stronger, the ankle is first immobilized in an synthetic or plaster cast. Once the swelling has completely disappeared, an orthosis (mobile splint), e.g. Aircast®, can be fitted. Depending on the results, training can be resumed after about six weeks.

> In the case of uncomplicated fractures, residual complaints, e.g. feelings of numbness, usually disappear completely.

The majority of malleolar fractures are Weber B fractures, often involving diagonal or spiral fractures about 1.5 inches above the lateral malleolus. Non-displaced fractures can be treated conservatively. The ankle is

SOCCER INJURIES

usually immobilized for six weeks in a synthetic or plaster cast. Sometimes, gentle therapeutic exercises can be introduced during this period. As long as the ankle joint is blocked by a cast, which prevents the muscle pump of the calf musculature from functioning, there is a danger of a thrombosis (blood clot) in the veins of the lower leg, which is why during the period of immobilization heparin must be injected daily into the subcutaneous fatty tissue.

When a cast is worn, regular anti-thrombosis treatment is required.

Displaced Weber B fractures require surgery. The fractures must be repaired with screws or plates. The advantage of this treatment is that it allows flexibility to be regained more quickly by avoiding additional immobilization in a cast.

Training Tip

Forwards and very young players in particular should wear shin guards that have a fixed, double-sided bone protector. They protect the ankle from direct kicks, but are soft and flexible enough not to get in the way.

Weber C fractures are somewhat less common. Here the point of fracture of the calf bone is above the syndesmosis (the ligament that connects the lateral malleolus and the shin bone).

In a Weber C fracture, the syndesmosis is always ruptured, and surgery is always required. In addition, the ruptured ligament must be sutured. Immobilization in a cast is then not normally required.

Medial Malleolar Fracture

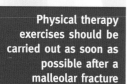
Medial malleolar fractures either occur in isolation or in combination with a lateral malleolar fracture. Non-displaced fractures are immobilized for about six weeks in a cast and an orthosis. Displaced fractures must be reset properly, then wired or screwed.

Posterior Malleolar Fracture

An avulsion fracture of the posterior malleolus (also called Volkmann's Triangle), is nearly always combined with a lateral and medial malleolar fracture. If the fractured piece of bone is small (no bigger than a quarter of the articular surface) or non-displaced, no surgery is required. However, larger and displaced fragments must be screwed.

Tarsal and Metatarsal Fractures

While both ankle and heel fractures are luckily very rare in soccer, metatarsal fractures are very common. In most cases, the fifth metatarsal is affected. The causes include twisted ankles and direct trauma, e.g. a kick from another player.

First Aid

Emergency measures are icing the affected area and taking the weight off the foot. If someone with sufficient experience is present, they may apply a compression bandage. The player must be taken to the emergency department immediately for an x-ray.

Therapy

Most fractures are non-displaced and therefore only need a cast. While for this type of fracture a lower leg cast is usually applied, in our practice we have very good results with a special synthetic-plaster slipper. This allows the ankle to remain mobile, so that there is no need for the chore of daily anti-thrombosis injections. However, the foot is well-protected by a strong, reinforced sole. If the pain is not too great, some weight can soon even be put on the foot. Depending on the x-ray results, immobilization lasts about five to six weeks. After this period, taping should be applied when training is resumed. Displaced fractures require surgery.

A special plastic synthetic bandage has proved to be the best treatment for a metatarsal fracture.

Toe Fractures

While big toe fractures can also be treated with a cast slipper, fractures of the other toes are generally treated by taping with an imbricated bandage. This involves splinting the broken toe by taping it to one or more neighboring toes (buddy taping).

In Focus

Take Care of Your Health

A soccer player's greatest assets are his/her legs, and treating them well will ensure a long sporting career. The knee and ankle never really recover from a severe injury; they will always be vulnerable. Younger player can compensate for this by developing strong musculature, but for players in their mid 40s, the situation is very different.

That is why every soccer player should question whether it really makes sense to dive in every tackle even if the ball is out of reach. Professional players are paid to risk their bones in the case of doubt. However at least at amateur level, health should always come first.

- Knee and ankle injuries are very common in soccer.

- Better coordination reduces the risk of injury.

- Mobile splints (orthoses), in which the degree of joint flexion can be fixed, are particularly helpful in the case of knee injuries.

- After immobilization in a cast, the musculature must be built up again with therapeutic exercises.

KNEE, ANKLE AND FOOT

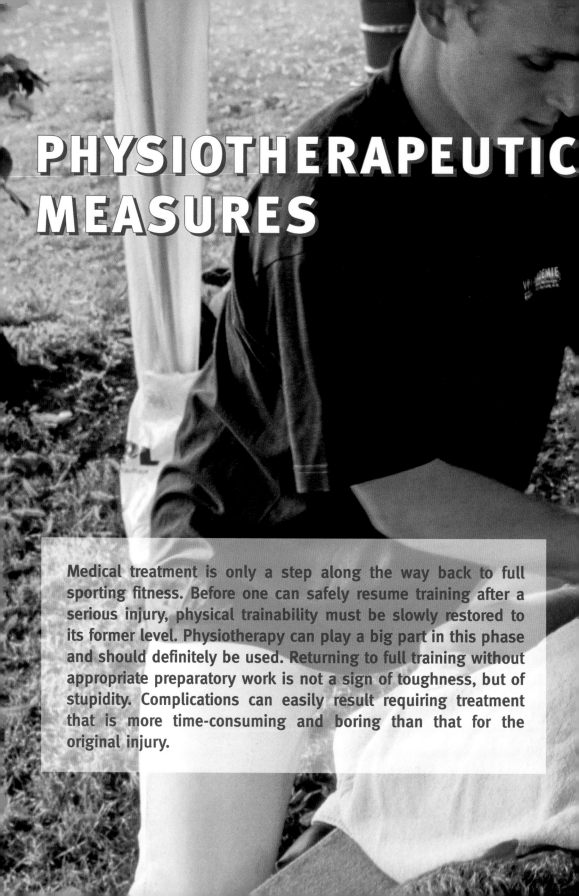

PHYSIOTHERAPEUTIC MEASURES

Medical treatment is only a step along the way back to full sporting fitness. Before one can safely resume training after a serious injury, physical trainability must be slowly restored to its former level. Physiotherapy can play a big part in this phase and should definitely be used. Returning to full training without appropriate preparatory work is not a sign of toughness, but of stupidity. Complications can easily result requiring treatment that is more time-consuming and boring than that for the original injury.

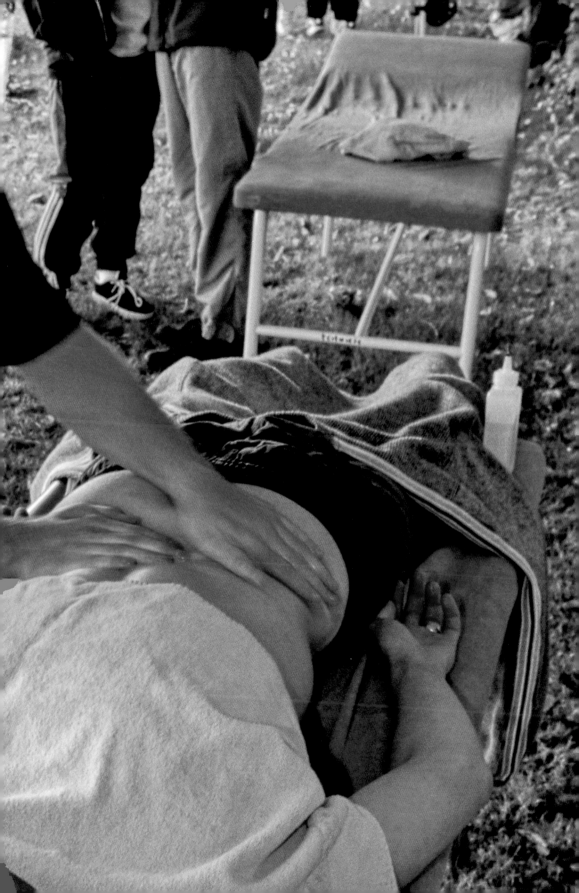

A good physiotherapist does not just try to restore pre-injury performance levels; he also helps the player to avoid similar injuries in the future. For this, he must have an accurate picture of the player's physical condition before developing an individual exercise program. This includes various muscle function tests, but above all an accurate analysis of any muscle asymmetries in terms of longitudinal growth or strength.

A muscular imbalance is often accepted as fate, instead of being deliberately overcome with compensation exercises.

We all have a "favored side". For example, the left leg may be stronger than the right, or the right arm may be stronger than the left. For the most part, this imbalance already exists at birth and is reinforced later on due to constant use of the stronger limb and an associated build-up of neuronal connections.

What may be helpful and useful in everyday life can become problematic after years of one-sided long-term loading like playing soccer. This factor alone can cause a variety of possible injuries. Innate deformities like bow-leggedness or knock-knees are more vulnerable to acute and especially chronic injuries.

Proprioceptive Training

Proprioception (in Latin: self perception), means the perception of physical movements in relation to the surrounding space, which can be recruited very quickly when required. Sensory cells in the muscles and joints work as receptive and storage organs. Proprioception can be improved by special training, e.g. with a balance board or therapy top. Studies show that targeted proprioceptive training can reduce the injury rate of the lower extremities in soccer players.

SOCCER INJURIES

Proprioception can be trained on a balance board. This reduces the likelihood of lower extremity injuries.

These deformities are not only an esthetic problem; they cause the misalignment of the bones inside the joint. In an ideal case, such misalignments should be corrected in childhood by an appropriate exercise program. It is really too late to effectively combat severe deformities in adults with a targeted strength training program.

In addition, over the years, wear and tear affects muscles, ligaments, tendons and joints, and its progress can at best be slowed, but never reversed. Don't let this discourage you, though! Measures you take now will determine whether you can still walk unaided in old age or whether you will have to rely on external assistance due to severe joint arthritis. You will still need healthy joints long after you have hung up your soccer cleats.

An individually-tailored exercise program can correct innate misalignments.

MUSCULAR IMBALANCES

A muscle works differently in different situations:

- It can perform an action itself
- It can perform a supporting function during a movement sequence
- It can have a braking effect, thereby making an important contribution to the protection of the moving joint or other muscle groups by preventing hyperextension

Exercises on the therapy top improve coordination and proprioception.

The main roles of these complicated muscle interactions are in complex movement sequences and the prevention of overuse injuries. To sum it all up, we can say that muscles do not work in isolation, but as a team, and this muscular interaction is called coordination.

If one member of this team is too weak, too strong or too short, the movement quality automatically suffers. A direct consequence of this is that performances that would be possible under optimal circumstances cannot be produced. In the long-term, all structures taking part in this physiologically unsound movement are damaged.

A crucial task of training is to improve coordination to a high level. The physiotherapist therefore creates the pre-conditions for the safe execution of intensive training loads, e.g. in the case of a quadriceps muscle in a cruciate ligament rupture, by concentrating particularly on those muscles that have a tendency to be weakened or shortened.

Commonly Shortened Muscles:

- **Chest muscles**
- **Back of the neck and shoulder muscles**
- **Hand flexor muscles (inside of the forearm)**
- **Lower long back extensor muscles (lumbar spine)**
- **Hip-lumbar muscles (transition to groin and thigh)**
- **Inner thigh muscles (adductors)**
- **Rear of the thigh (hamstrings)**
- **Shin muscles**
- **Calf muscles**

Shortened muscles are often the weakest link in the movement chain and can, like imbalances, cause muscles, tendons or ligaments to be unphysiologically stressed. If the physiotherapist notices muscle shortening, he will prescribe a targeted flexibility training program (stretching exercises).

Often stretching exercises alone are not enough though, for contrary to popular opinion, shortened muscles can also be too weak and therefore also need to be strengthened. A full range of movement should be aimed for. Muscles that are not strengthened over the full range of movement tend to shorten even more. However, full amplitude strength training does also benefit flexibility.

Commonly Weakened Muscles:

- **Shoulder girdle muscles**
- **Trapezius muscle**
- **Back extensor in the chest area**
- **Complete abdominal muscle loop**
- **Gluteal muscles**
- **Knee extensor / quadriceps muscles**
- **Shinbone muscles**
- **Foot muscles**

These commonly weakened muscles must be deliberately strengthened against resistance through the full range of movement if they are not strong enough. This is especially true for the abdominal and gluteal muscles. Both muscle groups have an absolutely vital role to play in soccer for explosive strength and trunk stability.

SOCCER INJURIES

MUSCLE TRAINING

Seeing a physical therapist represents a transition in one's sporting life, and it means that one must start to take responsibility for one's own body.

A compact but regular strength training workout should take place twice a week for the purposes of injury prevention. Have your physical therapist show you a couple of exercises or take advantage of the many possibilities of a modern gym. However, do make sure you receive individual attention and do not just let yourself be forced into a generic fitness program. You must work quite specifically on the musculature that you want to protect from further injury and whose development will boost your playing ability.

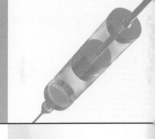

Strong muscles are vital for the prevention of injury.

Medical Tip

Older players in particular benefit from an important side-effect of strength training: a growth in muscle tissue has a positive effect on general fitness. Among other things, the fat and glucose metabolisms are stimulated. In addition, it is easier to maintain your weight if you have built up a lot of muscle tissue.

Soccer players live on their legs. In contrast to the unfortunately still widespread belief, strong muscles do not slow you down; they make you quicker and more explosive. So do not worry if your legs get a little more shapely, just think that every extra fraction of an inch of musculature increases the protection for your sensitive knee joint. You will certainly not gain large muscles anyway.

Squats strengthen the leg musculature, thereby offloading problem areas like the knees or Achilles tendons.

Quadriceps

The quadriceps has four muscle sections, whose profile is visibly seen in people with sufficiently low body fat ratio. The inner and outer muscles (m. vastus medialis and vastus lateralis) are particularly important for the stability of the knee joint. These areas should be developed when training the quadriceps by performing complex exercises like squats and leg extensions.

Hamstrings

The hamstrings (at the back of the thigh) can also benefit from intensive training. Along with the gluteal muscles, they are responsible for fast accelerations. This area must also be stretched well, though. These muscles are particularly prone to shortening and injury.

A shortened hamstring muscle spells danger for the knee joint.

Glutes

A firm posterior is not only esthetically pleasing, it also has athletic advantages. When it comes to running and jumping, the center of power is in the glutes. Squats or lunges ensure a rapid strength gain. Full squats are one of the most effective exercises that strength training has to offer.

Training Tip

If you already have the feeling in an unloaded squat that you are going to fall backward because shortened calf muscles mean you have to raise your heels from the floor, you should place a disk or a piece of wood under your heels. This will give you stability while you carry out the exercise. Stretch your calves so that you can soon squat without assistance.

If you have a history of problems with your kneecap or patellar ligament, the classic squat should be avoided. The pushing forward movement of the lower leg during the downward movement of this exercise puts excessive stress on the knee.

Back Extensors

The main role of the back extensors is to stabilize the spine. The backbone has to withstand a lot in soccer – from frontal collisions with the opponent to crash landings on the field. Hyperextensions are a particularly good way of training the back extensors, but make sure you execute the movement correctly. The spine is rolled from bottom to top. Hyperextensions with a straight back are a therapeutic exercise. In our opinion, healthy spines should be trained in a completely different way to injured ones. In practice this means that the musculature around a naturally very flexible spine must also be trained dynamically and not just statically.

Shoulder Girdle

Strong shoulders allow for greater dynamism when heading the ball. The shoulder girdle includes more than just the shoulders. In many people, the back part of the shoulder muscle and the so-called trapezius muscle (which extends from the back of the neck to the thoracic spine) are particularly prone to weakness. This area in particular is not so easy to train without dumbbells and machines. If they are not available, you can also use Tubes (fitness bands with handles).

THE FEAR FACTOR

Your body may have recovered long ago, but every time you touch the ball, the fear of another injury is at the back of your mind, which stops you from moving freely and actually increases the risk of further injury. You should therefore already start thinking about the psychological part of your treatment in the acute phase.

Along with the fear of renewed injury or pain, unrealistic expectations of the convalescence process can also have a negative effect. The human body is not a machine. Healing processes take time. Players whose self-confidence is derived mainly from their physical achievements are particularly prone to having unreasonable expectations. It is very hard for them to regain their previous form after a prolonged injury. The temporary drop in performance is often accompanied by self-doubt and dwindling self-confidence. The physician does not really have time to deal with the mental state of every patient. Even those close to the injured player can sometimes react impatiently if they must constantly act as a buffer for the player's mood swings. This is obviously not the best preparation for a quick return to the normal playing routine.

An experienced sports psychologist can be an important complement to doctors, coaches and the family environment in the mental recovery process that should run in parallel to the physical one, thus enabling previous performance levels to be regained. They are the missing link between an injured player and their immediate environment. A sports psychologist can ensure that motivation and rehab processes are moving in the same direction. They also have a whole range of measures to help with targeted fear control.

Treatment by a sports psychologist and the rehabilitation process must complement each other meaningfully.

In Focus

Well-protected

The musculature plays an important role in injury prevention. Muscles support and protect vulnerable structures like joints, tendons and ligaments. The stronger and more efficient the muscles and the better the general fitness, the better the body can cope with the normal stresses and strains of a game: tackles, twisted ankles, abrupt stops, etc. Conversely, these stresses and strains arrive almost completely unfiltered at the passive musculoskeletal system if the muscles are not sufficiently trained. However, this does not mean that you should hit the gym recklessly. You need expert guidance and a strength training program that promotes the functional development of the muscles that are important in soccer.

SOCCER INJURIES

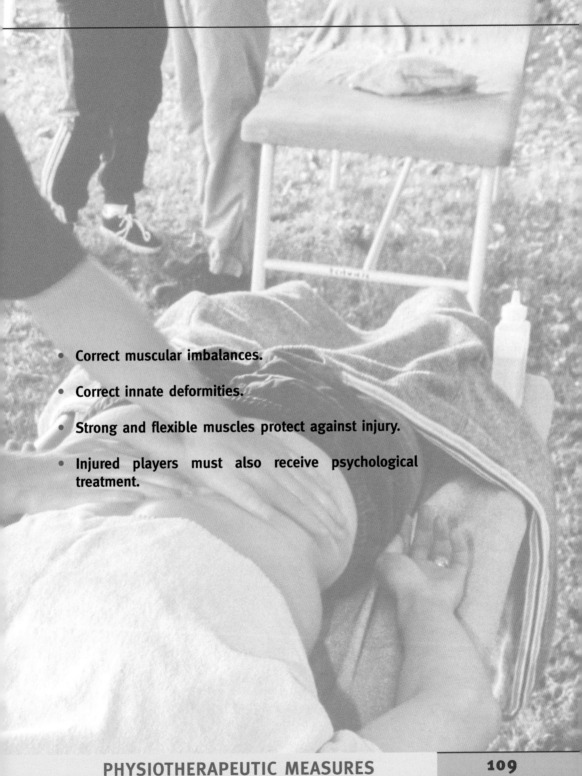

- Correct muscular imbalances.

- Correct innate deformities.

- Strong and flexible muscles protect against injury.

- Injured players must also receive psychological treatment.

EQUIPMENT AND EMERGENCY PROCEDURES

The medical equipment kept at the side of the field should be reduced to the bare essentials. Even a stretcher is hard to find in an emergency. Non-medical staff should in case of doubt only administer first aid and leave all other treatment to an experienced emergency physician. This greatly reduces the contents of a first aid kit, which should only contain what can be used without medical training. For non-medical team staff, the rule is: it doesn't matter how dramatic the injury looks to you, stay calm and confident. A displaced fracture or copiously bleeding wound may look alarming, but it does not help the affected player if you panic.

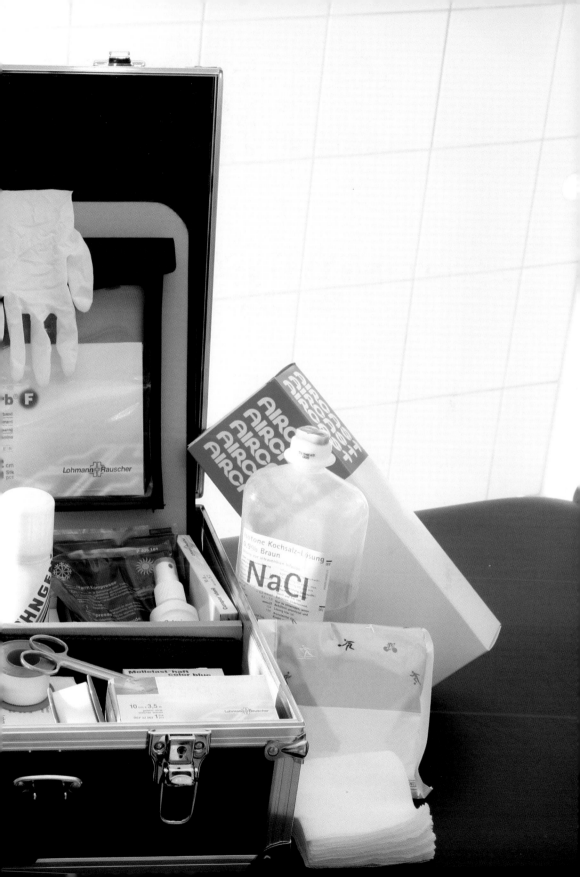

ALWAYS WELL-EQUIPPED

The materials and items of equipment listed below should always be on hand during training and for every game.

Contents of a First Aid Kit

- Sterile band-aids

- Sterile gauze compress

- Elastic self-adhesive tape (to fix bandages or band-aids over the wound, which would otherwise easily slip off due to strong sweating)

- Elastic bandages (in at least two different widths: 2 inch and 4 inch)

- Tape in 1 inch and 2 inch widths

- Tape scissors

- Disposable gloves

- Triangular bandages

- Possibly skin adhesive (to close small lacerations, e.g. Dermabond® or Histoacryl®)

- Possibly a stapler (to close wounds rapidly)

- Cool packs or ice packs (the latter need only be bent for it to cool automatically, so that no cooler bag is necessary)

- Ice spray (should only be used for superficial skin abrasions for pain relief; for muscle

injuries the cold does not go deep enough into the tissue)

- Disinfectant spray, e.g. Octenisept® (does not sting the wound)

- Saline solution to clean wounds

- Ankle joint orthoses, e.g. Aircast®

- Wrist orthoses e.g. epX-wrist band

- Analgesic, e.g. Novalgin

- Creams for sprains, bruises, blood effusions, e.g. Heparin cream

A correctly stocked first aid kit should always be on hand

RICE Rule

The correct emergency measures for most sports injuries are best expressed by the so-called RICE rule:

R = Rest
Until the injury has been accurately diagnosed, the injured player must stop playing or training immediately. If possible, the injured part of the body must be immobilized.

I = Ice

The thickness of the injured musculature determines the duration of the icing process. In general, icing should penetrate deeply and be long-lasting.

The injured area must be iced as soon as possible. The ice constricts the blood vessels, so that bleeding and swelling disappear more quickly. Cool packs or icepacks also alleviate the pain, and as the cold slows down the metabolism, it also stops the tissue damage from spreading. Never place the icepack directly on the skin, but place a towel or compression bandage in between. If no special ice pack is at hand, simple cold compresses will suffice.

C = Compression
A pressure bandage is applied to extremities with a tendency to swell and for joints after contusion, strains or bruising.

A pressure bandage is applied with moderate tension

E = Elevation

The injured body area is elevated so that the blood supply is reduced more quickly and to evacuate the fluids that have escaped into the surrounding tissue. This helps to reduce the swelling and the pain that goes with it.

PRACTICE FOR EMERGENCIES

Life-threatening injuries are extremely rare in soccer, but cannot be ruled out completely. If two heavy athletes collide awkwardly when running flat out, severe head injuries can result, in which case every second counts.

Medical Tip

Remember that first aid saves lives. As many people are not sure what to do, these simple measures are often not taken. This is why you should attend a first aid course where you will be shown which measures to use in emergency situations to save lives. If your last first aid course was some time ago, it is a good idea to take a refresher course.

As extreme situations are rare in soccer, they are usually very stressful for medical staff. The most important measures must be practiced regularly so that even under these conditions everyone knows what they are doing. A fast and logical response is required, particularly in the case of serious cardio-vascular problems and profusely bleeding arterial injuries.

Below there is a brief overview of the most important life-saving measures. This is only intended as a guide and should not be considered as a substitute for a practical training course.

An initial evaluation of the situation using a so-called diagnostic block:

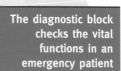

The diagnostic block checks the vital functions in an emergency patient

1. Check Consciousness

Speak loudly to the player, shake him/her by the shoulder or pinch under his/her arm (pain stimulus). If the player does not react, they are unconscious. This is a life-threatening situation. Call the emergency services immediately.

2. Check Breathing

As the musculature relaxes when consciousness is lost, there is a danger of swallowing the tongue and blocking respiration. The first step is therefore to free the airways. If the patient is breathing after this, lay him/her in the recovery position (see page 118). Respiratory arrest or gasping for breath indicates a danger of oxygen deficiency.

3. Check Pulse/Circulation

Take the pulse of the carotid artery in the left then the right wrist for no more than 10 seconds. As lay people tend to make mistakes with the pulse reading, general signs of circulatory function should also be considered (e.g. swallowing or moving). If there are no vital signs, start cardio-pulmonary resuscitation (cardiac massage and mouth-to-mouth resuscitation).

In parallel with these measures, always call 911. Never forget this number. Inform the emergency coordination center briefly and concisely of the circumstances of the accident and the player's condition.

Questions to Know in an Emergency

- **Where did the accident take place?**
- **What happened?**
- **How many people are injured?**
- **Which injuries or symptoms do they have?**
- **Wait for further questions from the emergency coordination center**

Cardiovascular and / or Respiratory Arrest

- Check for consciousness by speaking loudly to the patient. If he/she does not react, try to provoke a pain response (e.g. under the arm or at the root of the nose. Injured players should not be shaken after an accident.

- Lay the injured player flat on the ground. Tilt the head back carefully, holding the jaw bones with the finger tips in order to prevent the tongue from slipping down the throat and blocking the airways. Examine the throat and free the oral cavity from vomit or foreign bodies.

Use disposable gloves when examining the throat and oral cavity of an unconscious player.

In this position, check the breathing regularly until the emergency physician arrives:

- Does the chest rise?

- Does the player exhale?

- Is the breathing audible?

Recovery Position

The recovery position is used if someone is unconscious, but still breathing. It keeps the airways free and vomit or blood can run out easily as the head is now the lowest part of the body.

- **Kneel to the left of the unconscious person. Raise their left hip slightly and push their left arm as far as possible underneath their body.**

- **Bend their left leg and place their left foot near their bottom.**

- **Grip their right shoulder with one hand and their right hip with the other hand. Pull the patient carefully and gently to the left.**

- **Grip the patient's left elbow and pull their left arm carefully from under their body. The patient should now be lying on their left shoulder.**

- **Take ahold of their head at the forehead and chin and bend it down toward their neck. Turn their face toward the ground and open their mouth.**

If no respiratory activity can be detected, start to administer artificial respiration:

- Place one hand on the forehead of the injured person and hold the nose closed with two fingers

- Place the other hand on the patient's chin and hyperextend the neck so that the head tips slightly backward

- Take a deep breath and press your lips on the slightly open mouth of the injured player

- Blow air hard into the mouth of the patient

If you have done everything right, the chest of the patient should now rise. If this does not happen, you have not blown enough air into their mouth. Make sure that there is no gap between your lips and the patient's mouth when you blow and that the patient's head is tilted far enough backwards.

Repeat the artificial respiration process in a regular rhythm until the emergency physician arrives. If the patient starts to breathe before he arrives, place him/her in the recovery position.

Pulse Monitoring

If consciousness has been lost it is often difficult to establish whether the patient's heart is still beating. A very flat pulse is barely detectable at the wrist, especially for a medical caregiver who is under increasing stress. Do not waste any unnecessary time;

Artificial respiration should prevent the patient's body from being damaged by a lack of oxygen.

touch the Adam's apple with your fingertips in the depression near the windpipe (carotid artery). If no pulse is detectable at this point you must try to reactivate the heart again by means of cardiac massage.

- Uncover the player's chest.

- Look for the right pressure point: place the heel of one hand in the middle of the lower sternum.
- Place the heel of the other hand on top of the first hand, and raise your fingers so that you do not press down on the ribs.
- Push down strongly on the chest while keeping your arms straight. If the chest does not "give" about 4-5 cm, you need to push harder.
- Repeat the pressing movement about 100 times per minute.
- If cardiac massage and mouth-to-mouth resuscitation are required at the same time, share the work with a coach or another player so that you do not break the rhythm. The correct ratio of cardiac massage to mouth-to-mouth resuscitation is 15:2.

Continue with the cardiac massage until the emergency physician arrives, checking the pulse of the patient regularly as you do so.

Profuse Arterial Bleeding

We have already dealt with the first aid for bleeding that occurs in connection with skin or muscle injuries. The bleeding from an injured artery is more dramatic and the

SOCCER INJURIES

blood loss can quickly become life-threatening. Quick, decisive treatment is therefore of utmost importance.

- Push a sterile cloth directly onto the wound. If no suitable bandage is on hand, use your hand to press hard on the wound until the emergency physician takes over.

- Smaller wounds can also be bound. Do not remove a bloody cloth to replace it with another one; just bind the new one on top of the old one. As you do so, use enough pressure to make the bleeding stop. Do not worry about the extremities dying; there is not enough time for this before the emergency physician arrives. You can therefore never press too hard, only too little. Your priority is to stop the bleeding.

- The bleeding is automatically reduced if the affected part of the body can be raised and the area underneath the wound iced with icepacks. To this end, the player should be laid in the shock position (with the head lower than the legs and the upper body).

Fortunately, life-threatening injuries are rare in soccer. The most important first aid measures should still be mastered, though.

In Focus

The Limitations of First Aid

The well-trained and experienced team doctor who sits on the team bench is unfortunately only a feature of the higher echelons of soccer. In most games, in emergencies one must just be grateful if a well-stocked first aid kit is available, or a medical attendant is present. Then the question arises, how well-trained is this attendant? Is his knowledge limited to a first aid course that he had to take several years ago? The treatment of severe injuries requires not only goodwill but also the right know-how and plenty of experience.

If you are not a medical professional but still act as a medical attendant, this is very commendable. In case of doubt though, admit it when you are out of your depth. Just grab your cell phone and dial 911 before it is too late.

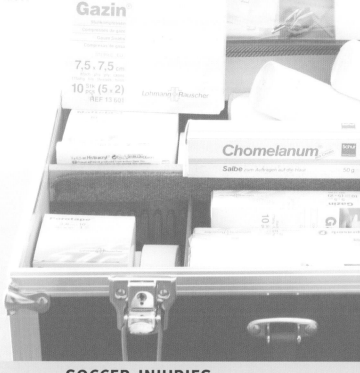

Check the contents of the first aid kit regularly

- **In the case of sports injuries, remember the RICE rule: rest, ice, compression, elevation**

- **Attend a first aid course**

- **Monitor the vital signs of an injured player using the diagnostic block: consciousness, breathing and circulation**

TREATMENT MEASURES

Small Open Wounds

- Clean
- Disinfect
- Apply a band-aid
- Place a self-adhesive dressing over the band-aid

Later on, check tetanus protection and change the bandage regularly

Larger Open Wounds

- Clean
- Disinfect
- Cover wounds with gauze
- Close the wound with tissue adhesive, staples or sutures

Later on, check tetanus protection

Heat Exhaustion

- Find cool surroundings (shade)
- Raise the legs
- Aim to cool a large area with cold compresses
- Ensure an adequate fluid and mineral uptake

SOCCER INJURIES

AT A GLANCE

Muscle Injuries

- Rest
- Ice
- Compression bandage
- Elevation

Tendon injuries

- Rest
- Ice
- Elevation

Joint injuries

- Rest
- Offload
- Reduce swelling with icepacks

Important: a dislocated joint should only be repositioned by a doctor!

Bone injuries

- Cover open fractures with a sterile dressing
- Rest
- Reduce swelling with icepacks

Photo & Illustration Credits

Cover design: Jens Vogelsang, Aachen
Cover photos: U1 – dpa Picture-Alliance, Frankfurt
U4 – Yavuz Arslan/imageattack, Witten
Adobe Image Library: 25, 33
Yavuz Arslan/imageattack, Witten: 18/19, 38/39, 46, 51, 63, 65, 72/73, 77, 80, 87, 89, 90, 93, 94/95, 99, 100, 104, 106, 110/111, 112, 113, 122/123
EyeWire Images: 11, 14
Daniel Kölsche/photoplexus, Bonn/Lünen: 96/97, 108/109
Lohmann & Rauscher: 44, 45, 48, 49, 74, 84
Ralf Meier: 21, 30
mev Verlag, Augsburg: 40/41, 54/55, 56/57, 70/71
Pixelquelle.de: 8/9, 16/17, 85
Andreas Schur: 37, 43, 69, 121
Sebastian Schur: 23, 85u., 114, 127
Side-notes: **left:** Chapter 1, 7 mev Verlag, Augsburg; Chapter 2–6 Yavuz Arslan/imageattack, Witten
right: Yavuz Arslan/imageattack, Witten

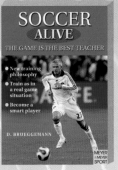

D. Brueggemann
**Soccer Alive –
The Game is the Best Teacher**

250 pages, full-color print
100 photos & illustrations
Paperback, 6 ¹/₂" x 9 ¹/₄"
ISBN: 978-1-84126-235-2
$ 19.95 US/$ 21.95 CDN
£ 12.95 UK/€ 19.95

Jozef Sneyers
**Soccer Training –
An Annual Programme**

312 pages, two-color print
More than 800 figures
Paperback, 5³/₄" x 8¹/₄"
ISBN: 978-1-84126-017-4
$ 19.95 US/$ 29.95 CDN
£ 14.95 UK/€ 18.90

Bischops/Gerards
**Soccer – Warming up
and Warming down**

2nd edition
136 pages, two-color print
22 photos, 172 figures
Paperback, 5³/₄" x 8¹/₄"
ISBN: 978-1-84126-135-5
$ 14.95 US/$ 20.95 CDN
£ 8.95 UK/€ 14.90

Ralf Meier
Strength Training for Soccer

128 pages, full-color print
100 photos
Paperback, 6¹/₂" x 9¹/₄"
ISBN: 978-1-84126-208-6
$ 16.95 US/$ 24.95 CDN
£ 12.95 UK/€ 16.95

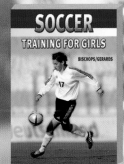

Bischops/Gerads
Soccer Training for Girls

160 pages, two-color print
20 photos, 70 figures, 2 tables
Paperback, 5³/₄" x 8¹/₄"
ISBN: 978-1-84126-097-6
$ 17.95 US/$ 25.95 CDN
£ 12.95 UK/€ 16.90

Bischops/Gerards/Wallraff
Soccer Training for Goalkeepers

168 pages, full-color print
89 photos, 81 illustrations
Paperback, 6¹/₂" x 9¹/₄"
ISBN: 978-1-84126-186-7
$ 16.95 US/$ 24.95 CDN
£ 12.95 UK/€ 16.95

MEYER
& MEYER
SPORT

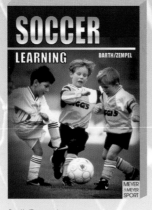

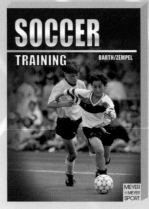

Barth/Zempel
Learning Soccer

136 pages
Full-color print, some photos

Barth/Zempel
Training Soccer

152 pages
Full-color print, some photos

Buschmann/Pabst/Bussmann
Coordination
A New Approach
to Soccer Coaching

120 pages
Two-color print
52 photos, 85 figures
Paperback, 5³/₄" x 8¹/₄"
ISBN: 978-1-84126-063-1
$ 14.95 US/$ 20.95 CDN
£ 9.95 UK/€ 14.90

Bischops/Gerards
Junior Soccer
A Manual for Coaches

2nd Edition
168 pages
30 photos, 67 figures
Paperback, 5³/₄" x 8¹/₄"
ISBN: 978-1-84126-000-6
$ 17.95 US/$ 25.95 CDN
£ 12.95 UK/€ 16.90

www.m-m-sports.com

MEYER
& MEYER
SPORT